WIN AT VIDEO POKER

Smiling players at the poker slots. (Courtesy Casino Player, the magazine for gaming enthusiasts.)

WIN AT VIDEO POKER

A Guide to Beating
the Poker Machines

ROGER FLEMING

A Citadel Press Book
Published by Carol Publishing Group

A Citadel Press book
Published by Carol Publishing Group
Citadel Press is a registered trademark of Carol Communications, Inc.
Editorial Offices: 600 Madison Avenue, New York, N.Y. 10022
Sales and Distribution Offices: 120 Enterprise Avenue, Secaucus, N.J. 07094
In Canada: Canadian Manda Group, One Atlantic Avenue, Suite 105, Toronto, Ontario M6K 3E7
Queries regarding rights and permissions should be addressed to Carol Publishing Group, 600 Madison Avenue, New York, N.Y. 10022
Carol Publishing Group books are available at special discounts for bulk purchases, sales promotion, fund-raising, or educational purposes. Special editions can be created to specifications. For details, contact: Special Sales Department, Carol Publishing Group, 120 Enterprise Avenue, Secaucus, N.J. 07094
Manufactured in the United States of America
10 9 8 7 6 5 4 3 2 1

Library of Congress Cataloging-in-Publication Data

Fleming, Roger.
    Win at video poker : a guide to beating the poker machines by Roger Fleming.
        p.   cm.
    "A Citadel Press book."
    ISBN 0-8065-1605-4
    1. Video poker.   I. Title.
GV1469.35.P65F54   1995   94-45524
795.41´2´028—dc20   CIP

TO MY SONS, BRUCE AND COLIN

I would like to express my sincere thanks to the following persons:
The inventors and developers of the Video Poker machine.
Paddy Gray, for inspiration and hours of chinwagging.
Liz Fleming, for her typing and retyping.
Mark Forshaw, for his belief in my book and my work.
Rob Hellings, for releasing the vital purse strings.
Tom Learmont, who translated the book from English to English.
Elaine, Paddy, Veronica, Pam and Mike, for patient hours of
proof reading.

Contents

A bank of video poker machines. (Courtesy Casino Player, the magazine for gaming enthusiasts.)

Publisher's Note

One has only to walk through the gaming halls of Nevada, Atlantic City, and the myriad (and proliferating) riverboat casinos to observe the increasing popularity of the video poker slot machines.

The book you are about to read . . . one which we believe will considerably increase your profitability . . . originated in South Africa. It uses the term **honor** to designate a picture card or a 10, that is, an A, K, J, Q, or 10. The use of the term may be different from what you are used to, but poker hands and their values are immutable throughout the world. As a professional poker player noted when he wanted to express an iron fact of life, "It's as axiomatic as a flush beats a straight."

Preface

Ever since I was introduced to the Video Poker Machine I have been hooked. The pleasurable hours I have spent playing have been an absolute delight.

I never really knew which option of cards to select for the second deal. I was not alone as everyone needs a guide to card selection. No book or reference was available so, being mathematically minded, I decided to do it myself.

Two years later, having analysed 2,598,960 different hands, I have the information I need. It is said that the very best Video Poker players have an error factor of between 2% and 4%. This book, if used correctly, brings this factor down to zero!

It is written in a no-nonsense, easy-to-understand style, enabling you to assess all the options you may take on the various poker machines. After all, you are not playing PACMAN. You're playing for profit and having fun at the same time.

I hope this book leads to many profitable hours of playing for you and increases your tally of elusive Royal Flushes.

Roger Fleming

Introduction

This book will be your passport to a great and profitable pastime. But before we plunge into the whys and wherefores, the probabilities, technicalities and tips, I'd like to take a leisurely overview of the areas we're going to explore.

Firstly, I didn't write for people who are good at math. If you're thinking: "I'm hopeless with numbers, I can never figure the odds," this is just the book you need. I use a new way to express the value of a hand. I don't talk about probabilities - instead, I boil your chances down to common sense dollars and cents.

I have designed the book to teach you slowly and progressively. There's no need to rush through the chapters; take them one at a time. Absorb the information at your own pace, building a solid foundation of Video Poker knowledge and skills. I suggest that you read a chapter, then have a session of Video Poker at your favorite casino, so that you can put your new-found confidence to the test.

Chapter One is a general introduction to the world of Video Poker. I take the reader on a tour of casinos, with a little history thrown in and a fascinating detour through technical developments in gaming. Chapter Two is the basic "back to school" lesson for those who have never played the game. This chapter is an eye-opener for those who have come from card poker, and THINK they know it. After laying out all the hands for you, and showing you how often they are likely to crop up, I move on to the various types of machine, and provide a few useful tips for the player. Then I spell out my method of giving each hand a value in dollars and cents, and explain our objectives. You and I are not hoping for a rare fluke, the one-in-a-million shot; instead, we build our winning records on hands that are dealt often. I explain "percentage play", which is aimed at bringing you out ahead at the end of the day, the week or the year—in the fullness of time. By steady scientific play, you are taking advantage of the theory of probability.

Chapter Three gets down to elementary playing tactics. I help you to lay down a solid foundation of skills and concepts, and put a few myths and misconceptions to rest. I weed out bad habits like holding useless cards and explain the importance of the redeal, which is your second bite of the apple. I also show you how to get more bang for your buck; money management, budgeting and stop-loss strategies. Chapter Four is our first day in 'big school', I outline your options with picture cards, in a chapter which solves plenty of puzzles. A Royal Flush may be a once-in-a-lifetime event, but I show you how to encourage it, if it's waiting in the wings. Chapter Five takes us out of high school into Video Poker varsity, with tactics for handling straight flushes. Chapter Six rewrites the rules; the odds change as a progressive poker jackpot rises. You should know when and how to adopt new strategies.

Chapter Seven specializes in the nature of the beast; how to handle different models of Video Poker Machine with different payout scales. Chapter Eight covers the exciting world of competitions and buy-ins, where Video Poker becomes a competitive sport and winner takes all. I know the joy of winning, and I tell you about it; but I also tell you HOW I won. Chapter Nine takes us right to the edge; adrenalin territory for the real risk-taker. In Chapter Nine, which is highly unscientific, my good friend Paddy Gray contributes an amusing picture of gaming superstitions. Then comes the fascinating quiz section; use it to test your progress through the book, and it will tell you how you're developing as a Video Poker Ace.

Now, if you're ready to take that first step, let me welcome you to the world of Video Poker.

WIN AT VIDEO POKER

A video poker slot. (Courtesy Casino Player, *the magazine for gaming enthusiasts.*)

WELCOME TO THE WORLD OF VIDEO POKER

Welcome to the bright eyed world of Video Poker. If you are a new player, you are entering a period which will give you countless hours of profitable enjoyment. You will play in magnificent surroundings, being waited on, and of course, by using this book, put yourself in the winning position. At the very least, more profits will allow you to play more confidently for a longer period of time.

To those who already know the Video Poker world, an even greater welcome to this book. You have obviously derived great joy from your favorite game, but believe that you need that extra bit of help in unravelling some of the card selections that have left you undecided. You will certainly get this help if you are serious about your play. If you use the information in this book correctly, get ready for the satisfaction of hunting for more Royal Flushes than before.

The Video Poker Machine is based on the Five Card Poker game which has been with us for generations, but beside the winning combinations, they are totally different games.

Success in card poker relies on skills such as mathematical probabilities, deception, card counting and an instant analysis of the personalities involved in the school. Unless you can combine all these skills and find fellow players, by appointment, you will have no joy in playing card poker. The good players always win in the end which leads to less players being willing to play with them. It is also possible to lose a hand in card poker simply by running out of money.

15

Video Poker, on the other hand, has no fellow players, deception or analysis to worry about. All you need is a keen knowledge of card selection. This will become second nature with enough practice.

The electronic age has encroached on the gaming industry which has really enhanced it. For many people, casino table play has been intimidating. They fear making foolish mistakes or feeling sheepish as they leave a table "skint".

Video Poker machines were first introduced in America in 1976. They took many years to grow in popularity, under-standing and refinement but once they caught on, they became a success story. The players increased every year and larger sections of the casinos were set aside for banks (rows) of Video Poker Machines.

The original machines did not work on credits and all wins were paid out by the coins dropping out into the metal tray. No opportunity existed to double your winnings and players were left with dirty hands by continually having to handle coins.

A Progressive Jackpot for getting a Royal Flush was in operation but, because of the cost of soap and the wear and tear of the machines, it only started at $1,500 for five $1 coins. The minimum today would be $4,000; some start even higher. Modern machines have better payout scales and jackpots.

Year by year the machines were improved and upgraded. The less attention the casinos needed to give them and the growth in their popularity resulted in more favorable payout scales and jackpots. Playing with a credit meter speeded up play and generated more turnover for the operators.

More varieties were introduced including a variance in payout scales and bonuses for achieving specific results such as a Royal Flush and four of a kind. Jokers and Wild Cards were among the innovations.

The modern machines are really hi-tech beasts. A single machine can be set up to receive any number of coins and pay out any variety of scales. Everything will be visible to you. There are no hidden tricks as is possible with reel-type slot machines. As we go to press, the total population of Video Poker machines in licensed casinos is rapidly expanding.

I prefer to think of Video Poker as more than just the thinking person's slot machine. Thinking person, yes - slot machine, no. The Poker machine uses a finite number of cards and they are electronically shuffled before each game. What you see is what you get.

The slant top machine has added to the general comfort of the player. This machine has the video screen placed almost horizontal to the floor. The choice of upright or slant top machines is yours for the variation in eyesight and posture while playing. Add their beautiful clean-cut looks and efficiency and it is a pleasure playing Video Poker today.

Imagine - all this development has taken place for you to create a world of your own. Just you and the machine. Gone are the days of card poker where you could play twenty games an hour. Now you can have over a thousand with no one rushing or slowing you.

Let's close the door on the card poker world and open up to the Video Poker machine. There are some card selection and discard tactics that you will have to leave behind. In exchange you will, at least, once in your lifetime see a Royal Flush, which card players rarely ever see.

The modern Video Poker Machine is all action. The machines linked to a Progressive Jackpot exude a new excitement. Not only do these Jackpots rise to extremely high amounts but for a *side-show,* some selected machines will pay One Million Dollars when you are *dealt* a Royal Flush in spades. Some side-show!

The highest Royal Flush payout available is $240,000 playing three $100 tokens. Outside of that and side-shows, I believe the highest Progressive Jackpot won in proportion to the initial stake has been $22,604 for an investment of five $1 coins. A return of 4,520 to 1!

17

In today's casino, comfort and excitement are the order of the day. Attendants are always available to serve you drinks, fix any glitches in the machine and pay you any excessive (if there's such a thing) jackpots that the machine cannot handle.

The innovations of competitions and buy-ins to find the most skilled players have added more glamour and variety to the game. You should get involved in these events because, even if you are not successful, your skill is improved and the camaraderie you will experience in mixing with fellow players is meaningful. Sometimes you may sink too deeply into an isolated world of just you and a metal machine. It is good to get out for a real experience.

Most casinos are continually running promotions. The reason is quite obvious in that they want your business. This is a win/win situation because every promotion puts you in line to win or, at least, qualify you for something extra. It makes sense to get involved in these promotions and choose the best promotion on offer. Healthy competition exists between casinos.

No money is spared in providing the most up to date equipment and making the casino as enchanting and comfortable as possible. The aim is to prolong your stay.

Part of the comfort in the casino is the sense of security. Beside uniformed attendants there are plain clothes security officers keeping an eye on things. It is widely known that a security control center exists where, by means of video cameras, an eye is also kept on proceedings.

The security protects the casino's cash interest. For someone to take illegal advantage of the casino would lead them to having to recoup the money from you and I by way of lower payouts. Casinos are businesses. Without making a profit, the casinos would not be there for us to enjoy.

That is the first advantage of security control. The others are personal safety and the rectifying of mistakes. Most people are unaware that if they are getting undue attention from an obnoxious person, all they have to do is report the matter to an attendant and the problem will be discreetly solved. So discreetly that you have probably never seen it happen.

If you still believe that security is only to protect the interests of the casino, let me relate a true story to you.

In mid 1993, I was at a casino having spent an enjoyable evening indulging my favorite addiction. It was about 3:00 a.m. and while I was sipping a cup of coffee, a breathless attendant approached me and asked whether I had cashed in some coins one and a half hours earlier at a particular cash-in point. I had, and I fitted the description he had received over his radio.

What had happened was that I had inadvertently left four full wraps of coins at the bottom of my tub of coins when I handed them in for cashing. This resulted in the wraps jamming the counter and I was short paid.

When this was discovered, my identity was picked up on video tape and the search began.

All I then had to do was stand in view of the camera where the control room confirmed my identity and I was paid out the money due me.

So there is integrity and protection for the player in casinos. I needed no more proof that the casino security department is for the benefit of both parties.

If you are a person who prefers, for personal and security reasons, not to be identified as a winner, play in the Salon Privé (available in many casinos). This is a section separate from the main casino where you can play in private. The denominations are usually higher but, with the help of this book, you can improve your skill and play there. There is normally no restriction to you being there as long as you are playing.

You will enjoy the world of Video Poker. Obviously, a good knowledge of card selection will add to your comfort and your pocket. This book is meant to do that. Read it, study it and keep it as a reference in future.

2 AIMS OF VIDEO POKER

WHAT MUST BE ACHIEVED

No matter how comfortably you are sitting; regardless of how pretty that machine looks in front of you, you are going to have to achieve some results or else you won't stay long.

The hands pictured below are the only ones that, if you achieve them, will give you a return on your money. Get familiar with them. Remember that the order of the cards on the screen does not affect the result.

Fig. 1

PAIR OF JACKS OR HIGHER

Any two cards of Jacks, Queens, Kings or Aces together with any other three odd cards.

Fig. 2

TWO PAIRS

Any pair of two cards of the same denomination plus an odd card. In Video Poker, there is no greater value in getting pairs of Aces and Kings or Twos and Threes. All these pairs rank equally.

20

Fig. 3

THREE OF A KIND (TRIP)

Any three cards of the same denomination plus two odd cards. This combination is more often referred to as a Trip, i.e. Trip Tens, Trip Aces, etc.

Fig. 4

STRAIGHT

This is any sequence of five cards not of the same suit (i.e. Spades, Hearts, Diamonds or Clubs). The Ace counts as a one or follows the King, but may not be used in the middle of a sequence.

Fig. 5

FLUSH

Any five cards of either Spades, Hearts, Diamonds or Clubs. They are also not in sequence.

Fig. 6

FULL HOUSE

This comprises three cards of one denomination and two cards of another, regardless of their ranking.

Fig. 7

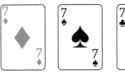

4 OF A KIND (PENALTIES)

Simply four cards of the same denomination plus an odd card. This combination is also popularly referred to as Penalties, i.e. Penalty Aces.

Fig. 8

STRAIGHT FLUSH

Any sequence of five cards of the same suit. In Straight Flushes the Ace only counts as a One.

Fig. 9

ROYAL FLUSH

A sequence of five cards of the same suit from the Ten to the Ace.

Remember again, that the order of cards in which the above combinations appear on the screen need not follow any particular sequence. This means that you must concentrate and keep your wits about you.

There are no other winning combinations. Card poker would rank four of a flush above four of a straight but that is to beat an opponent.

REWARDS FOR WIN COMBINATIONS

The payout of the machine is roughly in proportion to the rarity in achieving the winning combinations. As an example, listed below is the frequency in which you will be **DEALT** these combinations.

	Pr Jacks or higher	1 in about 8 hands
	2 Pairs	1 in about 21 hands
	3 of a Kind	1 in about 48 hands
	Straight	1 in about 256 hands
Table 1	Flush	1 in about 505 hands
	Full House	1 in about 694 hands
	4 of a Kind	1 in about 4,165 hands
	Straight Flush	1 in about 72,193 hands
	Royal Flush	1 in about 649,740 hands

For interest sake there are a total of 2,598,960 totally different hands that can be dealt to you. We may in future loosely refer to them as 2.6 million hands.

Obviously, the more rare the winning combination, the greater the reward from the machine and it will pay you out or credit you for later use or cash out.

Because machines vary in the multiples of coins they will accept, the returns are detailed as a return on one coin or token.

	Pr Jacks or higher	Money back
	2 Pairs	2 coins for one
	3 of a Kind	3 coins for one
	Straight	4 coins for one
Table 2	Flush	5 or 6 coins for one
	Full House	6, 7, 8 or 9 coins for one
	4 of a Kind	25, 40 or 80 coins for one
	Straight Flush	50 or 100 coins for one
	Royal Flush	250, 500, 800, 1000 or more coins for one

Studying this list will explain the relationship between their ranking and the rarity of hands. Unfortunately, in card poker two pairs will beat one pair as much as a Royal Flush will beat one pair. Only a few players will ever achieve a Royal Flush in their lifetime and instead of getting some huge pay-off, all they receive is the pot (which might be meagre). This is where the poker machine does justice to this imbalance. In Video Poker you are paid back roughly in ratio to the value of the hand you achieve.

The whole essence of poker machines is just that: a hand is valued according to its rarity. You will be rewarded in proportion to the risk you take. This must be borne in mind for as long as you play poker machines. In the same breath, it does not automatically follow that you should always try the highest risk. A lower risk may, at times, give far greater rewards in a session of play.

As with card poker, Video Poker allows you two bites of the apple. After the initial deal you may hold any cards and discard the ones you do not want. The machine will replace the discards with new cards from the deck.

> Please note that when a card is discarded, it will not reappear in the same hand.

Without assistance from a book of this kind, most players fall into bad habits. What happens is that they may hold the most outlandish combinations and, through sheer luck, end up with a winning combination. Being new at the game, this seems to make an indelible impression on them and they slip into very bad habits.

> The whole idea of this book is that you make the best use of your initial deal in holding the cards that will give you the best return in the long run.

24

One swallow does not make a summer! Any win is possible but, in the fullness of time, these bad habits will cost you dearly. Know when to hold 'em and when to fold 'em. We'll discuss examples later in the book.

At no time will we argue that any combination is unattainable but flukes are not, and cannot, be relied upon, together with the element of sheer luck. In fairness, you would not be reading this if you really believed in flukes and were not trying to improve your game.

HOW TO WORK THE POKER MACHINES

Poker machines differ in layout, but essentially they all have the same type of controls.

To stake your bet, insert coins in the slot provided for them. You may insert one coin or more as machines have a maximum of three, five, eight or more. Some new machines take a credit card and will register credits on the screen from which you can draw.

Once you have inserted the number of coins you are going to stake, press DEAL/DRAW and five cards will be displayed on the screen.

> BEWARE! Some machines, when you insert the maximum number of coins, will draw your initial deal automatically. If you inadvertently press DEAL/DRAW, you will discard your hand without the opportunity to choose the best cards to hold.

You may now decide from the hand you have drawn, whether there are any winning combinations and how best to improve the result with the next draw of cards.

At this stage you may discard any or all of the cards you have been dealt. What you actually do is HOLD the cards you do not want to discard. This is done by pressing the HOLD buttons placed in front of the respective cards.

25

To deselect any HOLD, press the same button again. Some machines automatically select the cards for you. BEWARE of this for two reasons. Firstly, by pressing the HOLD button you will actually release the card and, secondly, these machines do not always select the best options. We'll talk about this in another chapter. Check that the options selected are the best and that they are HELD correctly. Now press the button marked DEAL/DRAW. The discarded cards will be replaced by others and your final result will be displayed.

At this stage, most machines will offer to let you double your win. Arrows on the screen will point to YES or NO buttons. Press the relevant button to continue play. If you have a winning (paying) selection, the poker machine will automatically pay you out. Normally this is done by displaying a credit on the screen although sometimes your winning coins will drop into the payout tray. If you have credits displayed, you may draw from them to continue playing by pressing 1 BET as many times as the number of coins you wish to play. When you intend playing the maximum coins allowed, simply press the button PLAY MAX COINS and the cards will automatically be dealt. (Remember, again, not to press DEAL as the machine will immediately redeal for you and possible advantages will be lost.)

When you feel you have maximised the profit you have made, simply press the CASH OUT button to receive your coins. Sometimes the machine does not have the capacity to pay out large sums. In that case an attendant must be called to issue you with a voucher for the balance, which you can redeem at the cashier. Make sure, when this happens, that there are no credits left in the machine.

> The rules in this book only apply when playing the maximum number of coins.

26

CHOOSING A MACHINE

SHOPPING AROUND

When you go out shopping, you are always conscious of the value you are getting for your money. Admittedly, at times you may spend money on a whim for impractical reasons that are personal to you and bring you joy.

In a casino, when money for money is involved, you must do your shopping more shrewdly. Even some very seasoned Video Poker players have never noticed that identical looking machines have different payout scales.

I remember sitting next to a lady who was a fellow finalist in a very big poker tournament. We were having a chat and it transpired that she had never noticed that there were different payout scales. From that moment on she became a shrewd shopper and incidentally ended up as the top lady in the tournament.

Know your machines. Why play on a low payout machine when you might just as well maximize your success?

TYPES OF MACHINES

Outside of Joker and Wild Card machines, there are basically three families of Video Poker machines.
    **The first is the type that pays out a finite payscale without any bonus or progressive jackpots.
    **The second is the machine that pays out higher for selected penalties (4 of a kind).
    **The last model is one with a slightly lower payout scale but which has a progressive jackpot for the Royal Flush.
All three of these families of machines have players with preferences for them. The payout scales differ in each.

> Always play the maximum coins and if this is not possible, go to a lower denomination machine.

The reasons are honorable enough. The cost of running all the types of machines is identical. Naturally, to cover this, the lower denomination machines will pay out slightly less. This will encourage you to play the higher denominations—but that's life!

Whatever denomination machine you choose to play, check that the payout scale is the highest available.

It is a futile exercise playing less than the maximum coins in a higher denomination machine just because the payout scale appears better. You will curse the day you get paid a pittance for a Royal Flush.

Always be on the look out for these pay outs—the Full House and the Flush.

Other payouts to consider are the Straight Flush and Royal Flush. But because of their rarity, they are not as important as the former two.

By far the most popular machine is the one that pays out 6 coins for a Full House in return for one coin and is linked to a progressive jackpot. You, the player, are actually financing the rise in the jackpot but this is what dreams are made of. The jackpots can rise to very high amounts. On one Happy New Year's Day I won a jackpot of $22,604 for five $1.00 coins.

Now that you are aware of how the payout scales vary, I hope that you will shop around in future and get a better return.

> Always check that the payout scale of the machine you intend playing is the best available.

UNDERSTANDING THE LANGUAGE

RANDOMNESS

The whole book is based on the fact that the cards will be dealt to you in a perfectly random order. What is random? Random means that the cards are electronically shuffled and will be dealt in ANY order whether in the initial or redeal phase. This is what makes Video Poker so exciting. You can just as easily get a Royal Flush dealt to you on a *dead* machine or draw penalties on a redeal.

I am often asked whether the machines are *fixed*. My answer is that, besides assurances by the manufacturers, there is NO NEED TO! The payscale is designed to give a return to the casino. If they needed to make a greater return, all they would need to do is reduce the payouts.

All the Video Poker machines featured in this book are definitely random and the mathematics surrounding this fact is correct.

WHAT VALUE IS YOUR SELECTION?

For this section, we will use a very popular payout scale to explain value of a particular selection. Pictured below is the scale sometimes referred to as a 6/5 (i.e. 6 coins paid out for a Full House and 5 for a Flush). The Royal Flush is fixed at 1,000 but it is more usual to be connected to a progressive jackpot.

	Pr Jacks or higher	1
	2 Pairs	2
	3 of a Kind	3
	Straight	4
Table 3	Flush	5
	Full House	6
	4 of a Kind	25
	Straight Flush	50
	Royal Flush	1,000

Throughout the book, all selections are based on playing $1 per game regardless of the denomination. The actual machine you play could be a 25¢, 50¢, $5 or $100 version but for simplicity, all the results are converted to an investment of $1. Let's illustrate the theory with a practical example.

You are dealt the following hand :

Fig. 10

HELD   HELD

Now, holding the pair of Twos would convert into a Trip every 8.7 times, and into two pairs every 6.3 times, Full House would come up every 98 times and 4 of a kind every 360 times. These are interesting statistics but they have no practical value. Here's a better idea - calculate the value in Dollars and Cents.

This has been done for you. Taking every possibility into account (in this case 16,215), the value of holding the pair of twos is 79.3¢. This means that in the fullness of time, if you held this combination 100,000 times, you would get a return of $79,300.

Fig. 11

HELD   HELD   HELD   HELD

Let us now consider holding the four Hearts. The only winning combinations available to you are a pair of Jacks or Aces, or a Flush. This is again calculated using all 47 cards that could replace the two of Spades, i.e. with perfect randomness every 47 times you hold this combination, your results will be :

Flush	9 times
Pr Jacks or higher	6 times

The ultimate value of this selection is thus $1.09. (Just beware that this is not the value of all draws for Flushes, because of the Jack and Ace. There could also be times when a Straight and Straight Flush could be achieved.)

Fig. 12

HELD   HELD   HELD

Lastly, let us consider holding just the Jack, Ace and Ten of Hearts. The adrenalin starts pumping because we are now in Royal Flush country! But what is the value?

There are 1,081 combinations of two cards that can replace the pair of Twos. Included in your winning combinations will be a pair of Jacks or higher - 240 times; two pairs - 27 times; Trip - 9 times; Straight - 15 times; Flush - 27 times and one Royal Flush.

Multiplying your wins by the payouts and dividing the total by 1,081, you will value the holding of this combination at $1.40.

The summary of the three options is thus:
(i)	Holding the four Hearts	$1.09 per $1 played
(ii)	Holding J, A, 10 Hearts	$1.40 per $1 played
(iii)	Holding the pair of Twos	79¢ per $1 played.

Your selection should now be obvious. EVERY possibility is taken into account on a completely random basis.
There could easily be times when a pair of Twos produces penalties and the Jack, Ace and Ten of Hearts produces nothing. But that's not the message of this book. It says that, in the fullness of time, your average return will be as displayed in this example. Call it percentage play if you like.

LET'S PLAY!

SOUND ADVICE

Right - you know how we interpret the value of the selection of hands, and you've got the necessary confidence. This is the right time to issue some sound advice that will increase your return. Just as much as you shop for the best payout scale, you must play maximum coins at all times. Do not shop for the best payout and then reduce your return all over again. The last coin increases the Royal Flush payout appreciably.

As you become more practiced and enjoy the game, your play will naturally speed up. The control mechanisms of the machines are not checked every day and some HOLD buttons are not always as responsive as they should be. Check that the HOLD symbols are clearly visible next to your selected cards.

When you have finished your session of play and cash out the credits you have accumulated, make sure that the screen displays zero credits. A coin jam could occur to stop the coins being dispensed. An attendant should be called to rectify the problem.

Some machines only pay out a limited number of coins. If your total credits are above this amount, an attendant will give you a credit voucher for the balance. The same will also happen when you have the pleasure of clearing the machine of all of its coins.

When you feel the coin counter at the cashier has under-counted your coins, you have most likely left a coin or two in the tray.

The coin tray may appear smooth, but coins do lodge on end in the corners. Do not leave any profit behind—it is yours!

Lastly, when a light flashes above your machine, it usually denotes a big win which requires an attendant to give you a credit voucher. Do not leave your machine—the cavalry will arrive! In those heady moments of getting a credit voucher, remember that it is just for *that* win only. You may still have credits left to cash out or carry on playing with.

THE BASIC VALUES OF SELECTIONS

In the illustrations of the following hands, you will recognize some of the dilemmas you have faced.

SMALL PAIR

Fig. 13

HELD   HELD

Taking in all the possibilities, the value is 79¢ where there are no other options. Now let's look at the combined options you'll face.

ONE PICTURE CARD

Fig. 14

HELD

Holding just an Ace can give you every possible payout

33

available. This includes a Straight Flush because an Ace also makes up Ace, 2, 3, 4, 5 of the same suit.

Fig. 15

HELD

The Jack is the best to hold on its own. This is academic because you can only play with the cards you have been dealt and I'm not advising you to discard Aces. The reason is that there are many more Straights and Straight Flushes available (7 8 9 10 Jack; 8 9 10 Jack Queen; 9 10 Jack Queen King; and 10 Jack Queen King Ace).
The values are :

	Holding only one	J	47.6¢
	Holding only one	Q	47.0¢
Table 4	Holding only one	K	46.7¢
	Holding only one	A	46.4¢
Just for good measure, one10			32.2¢

The small pair is thus the better option so far.

HOLDING TWO PICTURE CARDS OF ODD SUITS

Fig. 16

HELD   **HELD**

Again there is a different value for which combination of honor cards you hold. By listing the values you'll see the pattern developing :

	Jack Queen	50.9¢
	Jack King	49.7¢
Table 5	Queen King	49.7¢
	Jack Ace	48.2¢
	Queen Ace	48.2¢
	King Ace	48.2¢

34

The higher your second card, the lower the value. This is because the higher card dictates and limits the possible number of Straights that are attainable.

HOLDING 3 PICTURE CARDS OF ODD SUITS

Fig. 17

HELD   **HELD**   **HELD**

The values are :

	Holding Jack, Queen, King -	51.5¢
	Holding Jack Queen Ace -	45.6¢
Table 6	Holding Jack King Ace -	45.6¢
	Holding Queen King Ace -	45.6¢

The small pair is still the best option at 79¢. A friendly warning at this stage - you may be inclined to think that the values for holding two honors is better (Table 5) and choose to discard the Ace in the above deal. Don't do it. Discards can increase or reduce the value of your selection, but I'll, of course, deal with this in a later chapter.

JUST FOR INTEREST

Now for some some common cards to which values are attached and held automatically. I say *automatically* because under *Advanced Play*, the face of Video Poker WILL change.

HOLDING TWO PAIRS

Fig. 18

HELD HELD HELD HELD

35

Here the only possible result is being left with two pairs, or drawing a Full House.

Value : $2.34

Here's a test of your luck; on average you will draw a Full House in just under every 12 attempts.

HOLDING A TRIP

Fig. 19

HELD   HELD   HELD

Full House or 4 of a Kind (Penalties) is the only improvement available.

Value : $4.12

You will convert to a Full House every 16 draws and Penalties every 23 draws. It is a longer shot than you may have thought so do not be too expectant every time you are dealt 3 of a Kind.

4 OF A FLUSH

Fig. 20

HELD   HELD   HELD   HELD

Pictured above are the basic four cards of a flush. The value increases with the number of picture cards in the hand :

	4 small cards	96¢
Table 7	- including 1 honor	$1.02
	- including 2 honors	$1.09
	- including 3 honors	$1.15

If you compare these values with the example in Fig. 13 on page 37, you will notice that the Ten is not an honor because a pair of Tens does not pay out.

36

HOLDING A PAIR OF JACKS OR HIGHER

Fig. 21

HELD HELD

At this stage the value of the discards does not matter as the next win would be two pairs and which two pairs wins is irrelevant.

Value - $1.51

To know where you stand in the luck stakes, this combination will convert with the following frequencies:

	No improvement	10 out of 14 times
	2 Pairs	1 in 6 times
Table 8	Trip	1 in nearly 9 times
	Full House	1 in 98 times
	4 of a Kind	1 in 360 times

I have given close approximations because it is hardly necessary to become more technical.

4 OF A STRAIGHT

We have two kind of Straights to deal with here. The first is when it is open ended. (Fig. 22) That means a card on either end will complete the Straight. The second in Fig. 23 requires a specific denomination only, between the top and bottom card.

Fig. 22

HELD HELD HELD HELD

37

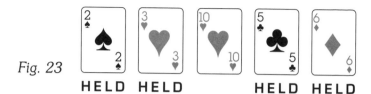

Fig. 23

HELD HELD   HELD HELD

Because there is an added winning combination of a pair of Jacks or higher in some cases, we will list all the values that include Jacks and higher.

	OPEN STRAIGHT		CLOSED STRAIGHT	
	4 small cards	68¢	4 small cards	34.0¢
Table 9	incl. 1 honor	74¢	incl. 1 honor	40.4¢
	incl. 2 honors	81¢	incl. 2 honors	46.8¢
	incl. 3 honors	87¢	incl. 3 honors	53.2¢
			J Q K A	59.6¢

Once again these are academic values because there may be better options available from the cards you have been dealt.

> To take advantage of reducing any errors, take note that a 1% advantage in a miserable hand is just as important as in a valuable hand.

LET'S ARGUE

Before we get into Advanced Play, there are some basic arguments to settle and some bad habits to rid you of.

THE HABITUAL HOLDER

Many people feel that when they are dealt a hand, there is some type of obligation to hold some card or selection of cards. But there are times when it pays to redeal—many times!

When there is nothing higher than a Ten that has been dealt, the first inclination to look for some card to hold, any card.

Here's a list of the values you'll get by holding one card. Let's presume that from Two to Ten there are no higher cards than the 10. From the range of Jack to Ace, the other four cards are between Two and Ten.

	HOLDING	VALUE
	Ace	46.4¢
	King	46.7¢
	Queen	47.0¢
	Jack	47.6¢
	10	32.2¢
Table 10	9	31.3¢
	8	31.3¢
	7	31.3¢
	6	31.3¢
	5	31.3¢
	4	30.7¢
	3	30.3¢
	2	30.0¢

> When you discard cards, they do not play any further part in the hand and will not reappear.

THE REDEAL

It is pointless trying to reform the *habitual holder* without demonstrating and talking about the redeal and its value. There are just 47 cards left from which a new hand will be dealt. The original 52 cards gave 2.6 million different possibilities. The redeal number drops to 1.5 million. A redeal improves the odds.

We must presume that there are still just as many Jacks and higher available as there were for the original deal, so the *deck* is richer in high cards.

Value of initial deal	33.1¢
Value of redeal	34.8¢

> Whenever any option is valued at less than 34.8¢ it pays to redeal.

REDEAL COMBINATIONS

Table 10 on the previous page tells you to never hold any single Two to Ten. In Fig. 23 you will also realize that to draw any inside card of a closed straight is pointless except when it contains at least one card which is a Jack or higher (A pair of Jacks adds to the value).

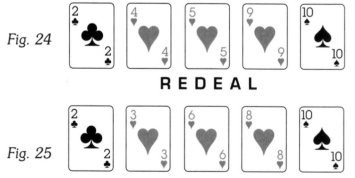

Fig. 24

R E D E A L

Fig. 25

R E D E A L

Although the above hands will give you a Flush, two pairs or a Trip, the overall value is low.

Value - 30.5¢

40

It is a 14% disadvantage not to redeal. This is probably the biggest single mistake made on Video Poker machines. Remember, this book does not say that any particular combination is impossible; with percentage play you will achieve a certain advantage or disadvantage *in the fullness of time*.

My method does not cater for the player who's feeling lucky and gets lucky. You must play the best percentages, to win over a period of time.

OTHER REDEALS

3 OF A STRAIGHT

Fig. 26

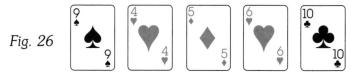

Value 27.5¢

2 OF A FLUSH

Fig. 27

Value 26.2¢

This is the worst possible hand that can be dealt. At worst there must always be at least two cards of the same suit. To hold them will quarter your money in time. REDEAL.

PAIR OF JACKS OR FLUSH

Fig. 28

HELD   HELD

OR

Fig. 29

HELD   HELD   HELD   HELD

The only way to decide this option permanently is to work it out logically.

Many people think that you have a one in four chance of drawing the correct suit to complete a Flush. After all there are only Spades, Hearts, Diamonds and Clubs making four suits.

What is forgotten is that four of the suit you are seeking are already dealt to you. So out of the 13 original cards there are only 9 left in the pack against 13 of the other two suits and 12 of the one being discarded.

Your chances are thus 9 in 47 which works out to a 19% chance. Multiplying this by your reward of 5 for 1 and the value is 96¢.

Obviously your pair of Jacks already has a value of $1 and can be improved.

      Actual Value   - $1.51

> Under no circumstances break a pair of Jacks or higher in order to hold four cards for a Flush.

Four cards is mentioned deliberately because later you will learn that sometimes you will break a pair of Jacks for three of the same suit.

42

THE KICKER

In card Poker, one of the techniques to disguise the value of your hand is to call for two cards instead of three when you only hold a pair. Your opponents are led to believe you are holding a Trip. The other reason is that if the odd card is an Ace, you may win a hand with a high Ace or two pairs with Aces as the highest.

Of course, this has nothing to do with Video Poker. Why many people hold a kicker is a mystery. Either they have converted from card poker or, when they first started playing, they got lucky and have never got out of the habit.

Where you have been dealt a pair, whether small or Jacks and higher, your next improvement will be two pairs. Of course, two pairs are two pairs regardless of which they are. If one of your two pairs is a pair of Aces, it may look better but there are no prizes for neatness.

Let the following table tell a story.

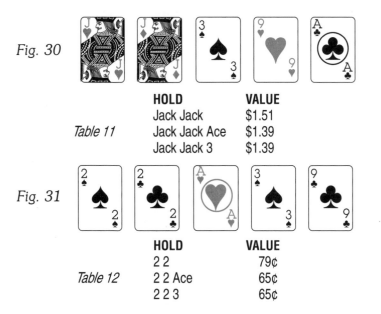

Fig. 30

	HOLD	VALUE
	Jack Jack	$1.51
Table 11	Jack Jack Ace	$1.39
	Jack Jack 3	$1.39

Fig. 31

	HOLD	VALUE
	2 2	79¢
Table 12	2 2 Ace	65¢
	2 2 3	65¢

43

Two observations stand out very clearly. Firstly, to hold an Ace or low card as a kicker makes absolutely no difference. Secondly, kicking a pair of Jacks and higher is an 8.2% disadvantage and kicking a low pair is a 22% disadvantage.

> Never ever hold a kicker or be seen by anyone else holding a kicker. It will eventually be more painful in the pocket.

4 OF A ROYAL FLUSH

Everyone's greatest ambition in Video Poker is to draw a Royal Flush. Some opportunities are missed through not knowing the value of being dealt four of the Royal Flush. Perhaps you don't see it because it is part of a winning hand and you don't know that it pays to break up *some* winning hands. The most valuable non-win hand that can be dealt to you is the 10 Jack Queen King of the same suit.

Fig. 32

HELD   HELD   HELD   HELD

Value $23.99

The lowest is four of the Royal Flush, when there's a low card of the same suit to discard.

Fig. 33

HELD   HELD   HELD   HELD

Value $22.47

44

It does not take an advanced player to realize that if these combinations form part of a Straight, Flush or pair of Jacks or higher, you should just hold the four Royal Flush cards.

Beware of the machines that will automatically hold cards for you. These combinations may be overlooked.

It is also hard to break up a winning combination when you are, say, playing maximum coins in a machine. This is understandable but you should either not be playing such a high denomination or you should take a deep breath and go for it!

Beginners: When dealt a winning hand that needs no improvement, press all the hold buttons next to each card. Then depress the deal/draw button to claim your win.

MONEY MANAGEMENT

A lot can be said on this subject. There must be some game plan that strikes a happy medium between going home penniless and being forced to go home with a fortune when the casino has to close. Both are finite situations but the second is very, very rare.

Firstly, the most basic mistake players make is to say that they are going to use a given amount of money because that is all they are *prepared to lose*. No one is prepared to lose and you are already in the wrong frame of mind to use that expression. Psychologically, it's better to know that you can *cope with the loss*.

You must take a finite amount of money along with you. Set yourself a target to win and be satisfied with it. There is no harm done if you exceed your target. If you then decide to play on with your *extra bonus* winnings, that is up to you, but if you lose the bonus, STOP!

One of the commonest expressions I have heard is *I'm playing with the casino's money*. What rubbish! There are never any refunds when you lose, so any winnings are YOURS. Play with the same discipline as if you had just started your Video Poker session.

It is very convenient to have credit facilities with the casino or to carry a cash card. Remember these convenience facilities would not be available if it was not in the casino's interest. No one will give you a stick to hit them with. It takes a great deal of self-discipline to handle these facilities.

If you ever once go over your *limit,* it is time to leave your cash cards at home. The saddest sight in a casino is to witness someone chasing their losses and losing more. Just as much as winnings are yours to keep, losses are behind you and are not recoverable.

In busy casinos, or busy times, it is sometimes difficult to

46

get a poker machine to play, let alone your favorite one. It is frustrating to run out of money once you eventually get a *good seat*. What a contradiction! If the seat was so good, why did you lose your money?

The temptation in these circumstances is to get far too many coins from the cashier so that you wait on line less and do not have to leave your machine early. The result is you draw the amount of coins from the cashier that you should in fact be cashing in at the end of a playing session.

I have seen players buying trays of coins from the cashier and I wonder what sort of vessel, short of a credit voucher, that the person would need if they made a profit. Doing this is the wrong way around, in my book.

Running out of coins is a natural barometer—it tells you to take a break. Being down financially can spoil your fun, and encourage you to take much larger risks, both in card selection, and the size of the bet of the Video Poker machine.

Video Poker machines seem to run in cycles of being alive or dead. This is all part of being random. These cycles can be of any duration of time. When is when is when? It is easy to presume that when you are initially seated in front of a machine, unless the display shows a player has cashed out, someone has just lost so you are now more likely to win.

You can have equal success on either machine. The machine could just as well have been in the middle of a winning or losing cycle. Many players find it more profitable to use one wrap of coins per machine until they find one that *understands their needs*.

The problem here is that sometimes it takes a long search to find a friendly machine and then you're reluctant to leave it when the cycle changes. The best discipline is to set yourself targets AND STICK TO THEM. Let's say you

47

have a credit of 150 coins; discipline yourself not to let the credits get below a certain limit. If your luck and skill continue, set yourself a new higher limit below which you will not drop.

It is very tempting when you have a credit of 300 to 400 coins to say to yourself that you are going to *go for the Royal Flush*. Don't kid yourself. First of all, the Royal Flush is not more available to you than normal and, secondly, on a five coin machine, you are saying that you have about a 15 to 1 chance of getting it. The odds are much longer than that.

When you are having a good run on a machine and sit back to reflect on how much you are up, those credits on the screen look so good. This is the critical time to decide whether to cash out or not. What may help your thinking is this bit of common sense. You have not won on a machine *until* you have cashed out. By the same token, you have not finished for the day until you walk *out the door of the casino.*

We have to be honest with ourselves about how much of an addiction Video Poker is to us. If you are satisfied with an hour's play, you are lucky and can usually play higher denomination machines but if you need a *fix* of at least five hours, you must manage your money in a different way. My best suggestion is to play the lowest possible denomination until you stabilize your fixation and then move to a higher denomination to play on the money you have left. If you end up *skint,* it's just as well you were playing the lowest denomination, isn't it?

> When you have accumulated a large number of credits on your Video Poker screen, you are actually allowed to cash them out. You don't have to use them up to zero!

LET'S PLAY SMARTER

FLIRTING WITH ROYALTY

There is no question that the attainment of a Royal Flush is the epitome of Video Poker. The payout is great and you are able to relate the success to your friends.

The more times you expose yourself to drawing for the Royal Flush, the better. It will come to you! You cannot chase this elusive hand. This section deals with the best options. Sometimes this will not expose you to the Royal Flush. It is futile to run out of money when the longer you play, the more chances you will have.

HOLDING THE 10 OF THE SAME SUIT

Let's put this dilemma to bed once and for all.

Fig. 34

The value of holding the Jack on its own is usually 47.6¢ and with the Ten it is 51.3¢. Discarding the Ten would actually bring the value of holding the Jack down to 46.1¢ because it removes all possibility of a Straight Flush or the Royal Flush. Seeing that dropping the Ten affects the value of the hand, let us analyse, in table form, what happens when you drop the other honors of a different suit, thus exposing yourself to the Royal Flush.

49

Table 13		ON OWN	WITH 10	DISC 10
	Jack	47.6¢	51.3¢	46.1¢
	Queen	47.0¢	49.9¢	45.8¢
	King	46.7¢	48.4¢	45.5¢
	Ace	46.4¢	46.6¢	45.3¢

The above table only shows that having a Ten and an honor forces you to hold the Ten. Also notice that the values with an Ace are the lowest, increasing down to the Jack.

> Under **all** circumstances when dealt a Ten and a picture card of the same suit, both must be held.

HOLDING TEN OF DIFFERENT SUIT

If the Ten and the honor are of different suits, the values are as follows :

Table 14		
	10 J	39.4¢
	10 Q	38.2¢
	10 K	37.0¢
	10 A	35.4¢

Holding the Ten, in this situation, reduces the value of the honors by between 17% and 24%.

> Under **no** circumstances hold just a Ten and a picture card of different suits.

HOLDING TWO ROYALTY

DIFFERENT SUITS:

Let us first see whether it pays to hold one or two royalty of different suits.

Fig. 35

HELD   HELD

50

The values are listed in this table :

	J Q	50.9¢
	J K	49.7¢
Table 15	Q K	49.7¢
	J A	48.2¢
	Q A	48.2¢
	K A	48.2¢

The values are identical again for the top cards. The top card dictates the value. Just to double check, the values of holding just one of the royalty, while discarding the other, are :

	J	46.0¢
	Q	45.5¢
Table 16	K	45.2¢
	A	45.0¢

> When two picture cards are available, hold both and not just one.

Discarding one honor has a disadvantage of between 9.7% and 6.6%. The only reason would be to expose yourself to a Royal Flush and, as you see, it is expensive in the long run.

SAME SUIT:

Fig. 36

HELD HELD

The values of holding two honor cards of the same suit are:

	J Q	62.6¢
	J K	61.2¢
Table 17	Q K	61.2¢
	J A	59.4¢
	Q A	59.4¢
	K A	59.4¢

The values are much higher than for different suits and you will obviously hold them both. Just to keep you in touch, the value of a small pair is 79.3¢ which is better still.

HOLDING THREE ROYALTY

We will now include the Ten in our Royal family to consolidate our thinking.

DIFFERENT SUITS:

 Fig. 37

HELD   HELD   HELD

With as little fuss, here is the table of values for holding any 3 Royalty of different suits:

	10 J Q	47.5¢
	10 J K	41.5¢
	10 Q K	41.5¢
Table 18	10 J A	35.3¢
	10 Q A	35.3¢
	10 K A	35.3¢
	J Q K	51.5¢
	J Q A	45.6¢
	J K A	45.6¢
	Q K A	45.6¢

In the above deal let us discard the Ten and see the results:

Fig. 38

HELD   HELD

52

	J Q	50.1¢
	J K	48.9¢
Table 19	Q K	48.9¢
	J A	47.8¢
	Q A	47.8¢
	K A	47.8¢

In every case, your value increases by discarding the Ten. This is an advantage of between 5.5% and 35.4%.

> When dealt a 10 and two picture cards of different suits, always discard the 10.

In Table 18, the values of the combinations containing an Ace look low. We've learnt that the highest card dictates the value of the combination. We also know that it lowers the overall value.

We discard the Ace and end up with the following values:

	J Q	49.5¢
Table 20	J K	48.3¢
	Q K	48.3¢

These values are higher than the equivalent in table 18. The J Q K left alone is of a higher value.

> When dealt three picture cards of different suits, discard the Ace if it is included in the three.

Doing this will improve your percentage by between 8.4% and 5.8%. This probably explains that feeling you get when you are dealt three honors and, although they look so impressive, you never seem to win.

SAME SUITS WITH A TEN

Fig. 39

HELD   HELD   HELD

The table of values of all combinations is as follows :

	10 J Q	$1.68
	10 J K	$1.58
Table 21	10 Q K	$1.58
	10 J A	$1.48
	10 Q A	$1.48
	10 K A	$1.48

This is the first example we have come across where the value is in excess of the R1 stake. Even though it is a non-win hand at this stage, if you were dealt this hand all day, every day, you would never have to work again. Now, let's look at the win hands that you are dealt, to see whether they have a lower ultimate value.

We will look at two possibilities—that you have been dealt a pair of Jacks or higher and three of the Royal Flush

Value of Pr of Jacks or Higher $1.51

Fig. 40

Comparing this value with Table 21, the pair of Kings is lower than the 10 J K, 10 Q K & 10 J Q of Hearts.

> When you are dealt three honors of the same suit, which includes a Ten, hold them in favor of a pair of Jacks or higher, except when an Ace is one of the three.

THIS WILL BE A DRAMATIC CHANGE IN YOUR PLAYING PATTERN. IT IS SO DIFFERENT THAT THE NEXT PAGE MUST BE MEMORIZED.

For simplicity, we will picture the rules you must observe.

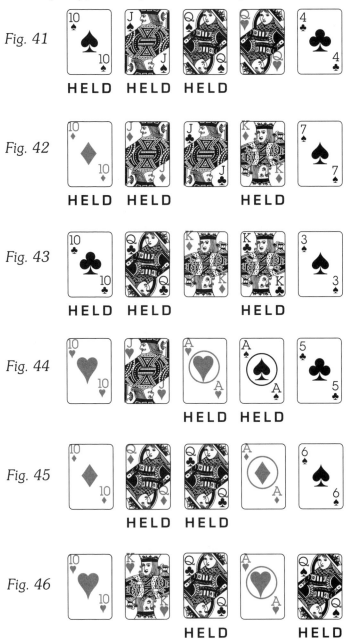

Fig. 41

HELD HELD HELD

Fig. 42

HELD HELD   HELD

Fig. 43

HELD HELD   HELD

Fig. 44

          HELD HELD

Fig. 45

          HELD HELD

Fig. 46

          HELD   HELD

55

SAME SUITS WITHOUT THE TEN

The table of values is as follows :

Table 22	J Q K	$1.68
	J Q A	$1.58
	Q K A	$1.58

All these values are higher than the value of a Pair of Jacks or higher.

> When dealt three honors of the same suit, **excluding** a Ten, hold them in favor of a pair of Jacks or higher under **all** circumstances.

HOLDING FOUR ROYALTY OF DIFFERENT SUITS

	10 J Q K	87.2¢
	10 J Q A	53.2¢
Table 23	10 J K A	53.2¢
	10 Q K A	53.2¢
	J Q K A	59.6¢

The values are determined by the number of Straights and pairs of Jacks or higher that can be achieved. Comparing these results with Tables 18 and 19, there is no way of discarding anything to improve the hand, even the Ten when the Ace is present.

HOLDING FOUR ROYALTY OF THE SAME SUIT

Have a good look at the most valuable non-win hand that can be dealt to you.

Fig. 47

HELD   HELD   HELD   HELD

The value of this hand is $23.79.

The lowest valued hand in this Royal family of four cards is:

Fig. 48

HELD HELD HELD HELD

This has a value of $22.47.

I said before that you must be careful that you do not just hold a winning hand when it is displayed on the screen. The only winning hand you would not break up is a Straight Flush, which has a value of $50. Break up all others.

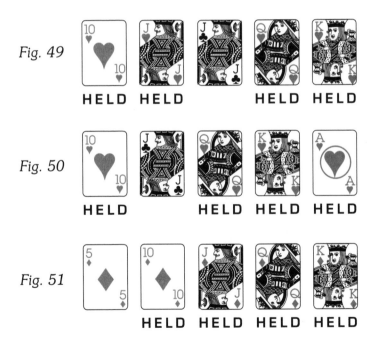

Fig. 49

HELD HELD   HELD HELD

Fig. 50

HELD   HELD HELD HELD

Fig. 51

HELD HELD HELD HELD

SPLITTING ROYALTY

Up to now we have handled the simple examples of all the Royalty being of different or the same suit.

Let me now solve a dilemma that very frequently confronts you. That is when you have either three or four Royalty and at least two of them are from the same suit.

Seeing that the Royal Flush is the ultimate single win, I'll give you all the best options. On one hand, we want to expose ourselves to drawing for a Royal Flush as often as possible and, on the other hand, to know when we are wasting money in doing so.

SPLITTING THREE ROYALTY

Let's begin with three Royalty of which two are the same suit.

THREE ROYALTY INCLUDING THE TEN

Because a pair of Tens has no payout value, let us start with the lowest values and work up from there. In the following deal we are confronted with a Ten of the same suit as one of the other Royalty.

Fig. 52

This time the table of values contains all three options which you can take, i.e. hold all three Royalty, hold the Ten and other of the same suit and holding the two Royalty which must then be of different suits.

58

Table 24

HOLDING ALL THREE		HOLDING SAME SUIT (DISCARD IN BRACKETS)		DISCARDING THE TEN	
10JQ	47.5¢	10J (Q)	50.2¢	J Q	50.1¢
10JK	41.5¢	10J (K)	50.2¢	J K	48.9¢
10JA	35.3¢	10J (A)	50.2¢	J A	47.8¢
10QJ	47.5¢	10Q (J)	48.4¢	J Q	50.1¢
10QK	41.5¢	10Q (K)	48.4¢	Q K	48.9¢
10QA	35.3¢	10Q (A)	48.4¢	Q A	47.8¢
10KJ	41.5¢	10K (J)	47.0¢	J K	48.9¢
10KQ	41.5¢	10K (Q)	47.0¢	Q K	48.9¢
10KA	35.3¢	10K (A)	47.0¢	K A	47.8¢
10AJ	35.3¢	10A (J)	45.5¢	J A	47.8¢
10AQ	35.3¢	10A (Q)	45.5¢	Q A	47.8¢
10AK	35.3¢	10A (K)	45.5¢	K A	47.8¢

The highlighted figures show the highest option for each selection that is dealt. Let us simplify this table by making rules for ourselves.

> When dealt three honors of which the Ten is the same suit as one of the others, never hold all three.

The above is obvious from the table so we are left with two more rules which actually complete this scenario.

> When dealt the Ten and Jack of the same suit among three Royalty, always discard the odd card.

> When dealt three Royalty of which the Ten is the same suit as the Queen, King or Ace, always discard the Ten unless the Ten and Queen, of the same suit, are together with the Ace, then discard the Ace.

We have tables and rules, but pictures tell the most, so here are some examples of best options. Let's become more realistic and jumble up the order so that you get used to the cards as they look on the video screen.

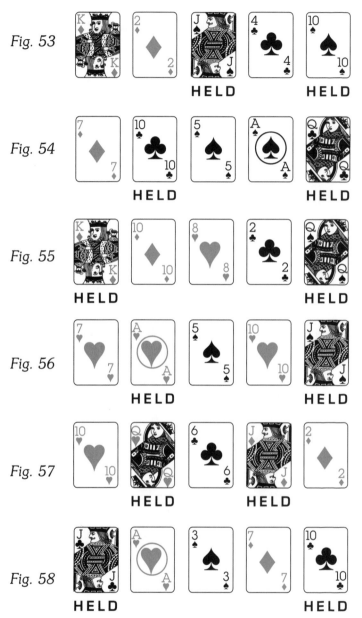

Fig. 53

Fig. 54

Fig. 55

Fig. 56

Fig. 57

Fig. 58

You can now select from the above with complete confidence. Let us move on.

THREE ROYALTY EXCLUDING THE TEN

We will follow the same format as the last, selecting all
three, two of the same suit and, just for the record, the
other two of a different suit.

Fig. 59

Table 25 may look a lot more involved than it really is.

	HOLDING ALL THREE		TWO OF SAME SUIT (DISCARD IN BRACKETS)		TWO OF DIFFERENT SUIT (DISCARD IN BRACKETS)	
	J Q K	51.5¢	J Q (K)	61.2¢	Q K (J)	48.3¢
	J K A	45.6¢	J K (A)	59.7¢	K A (J)	47.1¢
	J A Q	45.6¢	J A (Q)	58.3¢	Q A (J)	47.1¢
	Q K A	45.6¢	Q K (A)	59.7¢	K A (Q)	47.1¢
	Q A K	45.6¢	Q A (K)	58.3¢	A K (Q)	47.1¢
Table 25	Q J A	45.6¢	Q J (A)	61.2¢	J A (Q)	47.1¢
	K J A	45.6¢	K J (A)	59.7¢	J A (K)	47.1¢
	K Q J	51.5¢	K Q (J)	59.7¢	Q J (K)	49.4¢
	K A Q	45.6¢	K A (Q)	58.3¢	A Q (K)	47.1¢
	A J K	45.6¢	A J (K)	58.3¢	J K (A)	48.3¢
	A Q J	45.6¢	A Q (J)	58.3¢	Q J (A)	49.4¢
	A J Q	45.6¢	A K (Q)	58.3¢	K Q (A)	48.3¢

> When dealt three picture cards always hold two of
> the same suit and discard the other if it is of a
> different suit.

NOTE: Table 25 shows many combinations of the same
value. You'll notice that what they have in common is the
highest card held. Also, the higher the held card, the
lower the value.

HOLDING FOUR ROYALTY CARDS

We must next work out the best way of handling a deal of four Royalty cards of which some are of the same suit.

THE TEN AND ANOTHER OF THE SAME SUIT

Fig. 60

? ? ? ?

Before we split up these cards, let us establish the best value of holding all four in view of *going for a Straight.*

Value with the Ace	59.6¢ (Jack to Ace)
Value with the Ace and Ten	53.2¢ (Ten to Ace)
Value without the Ace	87.2¢ (Ten to King).

Any other option we take must exceed the value of the above to be more profitable.

Holding the two Royalty and discarding two others must have different values than before, so we have to make a table of values again.   As we have seen so far throughout the book the cards of the same suit we hold will differ in value according to their highest card. We will also simplify the table on the basis that the two Royalty cards discarded are irrelevant except when one of them is a Ten.

	CARDS HELD		BEST VALUES HOLDING THREE	
	10 J	49.0¢	J Q K	48.6¢
	10 Q	47.1¢	J K A	44.1¢
Table 26	10 K	45.7¢	10 J Q	44.2¢
	10 A	44.6¢	10 J K	38.3¢
			10 J A	33.9¢

From the above it is obvious that all four cards must be held as they are below the value of the Straight of 53.2¢.

> When dealt four Royalty of which the Ten and another card are of the same suit, always hold all four cards.

TWO OF THE SAME SUIT (NOT THE TEN)

Fig. 61

10♥   J   K   A♦   3♣

?   ?   ?   ?

The question arises again: Is holding all four cards better than two picture cards?

The table below reveals the values for holding all combinations of two picture cards and discarding the Ten and another:

	J Q	60.6¢
	J K	59.1¢
	J A	58.0¢
Table 27	Q K	59.1¢
	Q A	58.0¢
	K A	58.0¢

> When dealt four honors of which the Ten is one, and two others are of the same suit, always hold all four unless the Ace is included, then hold the two pictures of the same suit.

The value of the Straight starting Ten Jack Queen King is 87.2¢ and Ten Jack Queen Ace is 53.2¢.

Now that there are exceptions, it is well worth picturing some examples.

Fig. 62

HELD HELD HELD HELD

63

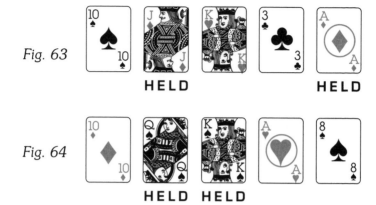

Fig. 63

HELD   **HELD**

Fig. 64

HELD HELD

FOUR PICTURE CARDS

Fig. 65

?   ?   ?   ?

Holding any two of the same suit and discarding the others leads to the following table :

	J Q	60.2¢
	J K	58.7¢
	J A	57.3¢
Table 28	Q K	58.7¢
	Q A	57.3¢
	K A	57.3¢

The value of holding all four cards is 59.6¢ so there is only one exception.

> When dealt Jack Queen King Ace of which two are the same suit, always hold all four unless the Jack and Queen are of the same suit, then hold only them.

64

Fig. 66

HELD   HELD   HELD   HELD

Fig. 67

    HELD   HELD

Being dealt four Royalty can be a bit confusing but, because you want to always take the best options, we will summarize all the rules in another form.

A commonly dealt hand is two cards of each of two suits. We have actually also covered this because the odd two cards could easily have been of the same suit.

FOUR CARDS	RULES
Jack to Ace	Hold all (except specifically J Q)
Ten to Ace	Hold all (except two picture cards of the same suit)
Ten to King	Hold all.

A Ten is never, under any circumstances, held with another of the same suit when dealt four honors.

> When an attendant pays you separately for a big win, check that you have not left any unclaimed credits in your machine.

65

FOUR ROYALTY WITH THREE OF THE SAME SUIT

Fig. 68

?   ?   ?   ?

This is again a hold-same-suit or hold-all situation, so let us list the values of three Royalty held, after discarding the fourth:

	10 J Q	$1.64
	10 J K	$1.55
	10 Q K	$1.55
	10 J A	$1.46
Table 29	10 Q A	$1.46
	10 K A	$1.46
	J Q K	$1.66
	J Q A	$1.57
	J K A	$1.57
	Q K A	$1.57.

The highest value of holding four Royalty is 87.2¢.

> When dealt four Royalty of which any three are of the same suit, hold the three and discard the other.

We are not finished yet! It is possible that we can have a pair of Jacks or higher in the same deal. The value of the pair of Jacks is $1.51 which is lower than some of the values shown in Table 29.

> When dealt a pair of Jacks or higher and three Royalty of the same suit, hold the Royalty unless both the Ten and Ace are part of the three.

Just to remind you! A good working knowledge of this section is imperative, so do not divorce yourself from splitting Royalty.

ADVANCED PLAY

You have learned the basics and have played smarter. This next section is for those among you who really want to be on the cutting edge and reduce the casino's advantage.

This chapter will need your concentration and memory to put the choices into practice. It does not promise to be easy, but if you are serious about money and Video Poker, and want to be a top player, you will have to know this chapter backwards.

STRAIGHT FLUSHES

Fig. 69

Straight Flushes are much more frequent than the payout scale would suggest. There are nine Straight Flushes to every Royal Flush in a deck of cards. We get them in that proportion for a couple of reasons.

Firstly, we value the initial hand dealt to us by first checking for a win, small pairs or Royalty. Often the options are not noticed.

Secondly, most of the cards held tend to be Royalty because the values are much higher. Two or three Straight Flushes for every Royal Flush seems a good average in practice.

I will first deal with a hand containing three cards which have Straight Flush potential and examine under what conditions we would hold them or not. Later analyze four of them to see whether these are worth holding.

Three cards of a Straight Flush potential can be separated into three categories. They can be consecutive cards in which case we call them *open*. There can be one gap in the three cards and we will call them *half open*. If there are two gaps, i.e. have the top and bottom cards of the potential Straight Flush, we will call it *closed*. With three cards of a *closed* Straight Flush there is only one Straight Flush possible. *Half open* can produce two and *open* can produce three possibilities.

With four cards it will be simply a question of an *open* or *closed* option.

THREE CARDS OF A STRAIGHT FLUSH

Let us start by dealing with low cards to ascertain their potential values without any Jacks or higher.

Fig. 70

OPEN STRAIGHT FLUSH POSSIBILITY

The value of this hand is 59.7¢

Fig. 71

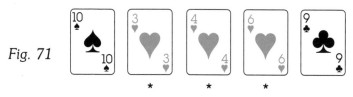

HALF OPEN STRAIGHT FLUSH POSSIBILITY

The value of this hand is 50.0¢.

Fig. 72

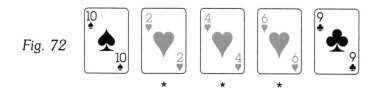

CLOSED STRAIGHT FLUSH POSSIBILITY

The value of this hand is 40.0¢.

Now that we have attached values to these three varieties we can see by their low values that there are many other combinations that we will hold in preference to them. Many Straight Flushes are not achieved because of this, but don't lose any sleep over it. You will only ditch them when a better option is available.

The value can increase when some of the possible Straight Flush cards are Jacks or higher, so let us look at a full table of values before we start comparing them to other options. Then you will be able to picture the possibilities for later discussion.

Fig. 73

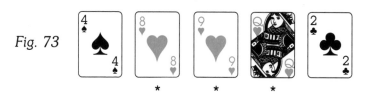

CLOSED WITH ONE JACK OR HIGHER

Fig. 74

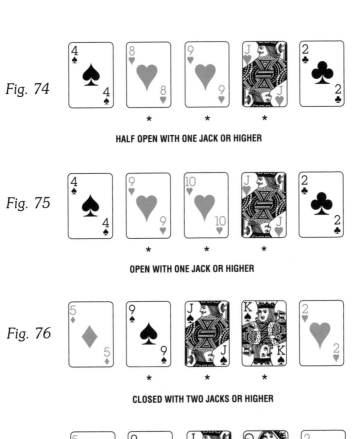

HALF OPEN WITH ONE JACK OR HIGHER

Fig. 75

OPEN WITH ONE JACK OR HIGHER

Fig. 76

CLOSED WITH TWO JACKS OR HIGHER

Fig. 77

HALF OPEN WITH TWO JACKS OR HIGHER

Fig. 78

OPEN WITH TWO JACKS OR HIGHER

Table 30

	OPEN	HALF OPEN	CLOSED
Three low cards	59.7¢	50.0¢	40.0¢
Two low cards + 1 Jack or higher	69.7¢	59.9¢	50.2¢
One low card + 2 Jacks or higher	$1.68	69.9¢	60.2¢

ROYAL FLUSH OR STRAIGHT FLUSH

Should you automatically hold the three cards, or discard any? Detailed below are the values of holding the Royalty on their own, singularly and in pairs. Only the relevant values are detailed, or else we are in Royal Flush country.

	J	46.1¢		10 J	48.8¢
	Q	45.9¢		10 Q	47.6¢
Table 31	K	45.5¢		10 K	46.4¢
	A	45.3¢		J Q	61.0¢
				J K	59.2¢
				Q K	59.2¢

The above values have to assume that by taking the Royal Flush option, you are closing the door to a Straight Flush and so are lower. Note that the Ace is only slightly reduced because an Ace can also start a Straight Flush. (A,2,3,4,5)

> When dealt three cards of any Straight Flush, **open, half open** or **closed,** including one picture card, draw for the Straight Flush even when the Ten is included.

Good! This also answers a dilemma you may have faced.

The following hand is interesting :

Fig. 79

HELD   **HELD**   **HELD**

71

A 2.9% advantage over holding the Ten and Jack. The above hand also holds for Eight Ten Queen (advantage 5.5%) and Nine Ten King (advantage 8.2%).

> When dealt three cards of a potential Straight Flush, which includes two picture cards, always hold for a Straight Flush except when it is **closed** and has the Jack and Queen; then hold them.

The Straight Flush opportunity containing two picture cards among the three is a very close shave as you can see by the table, but only when it is a potential Straight Flush. We're really splitting hairs in this case.

FLUSH OR STRAIGHT FLUSH

Fig. 80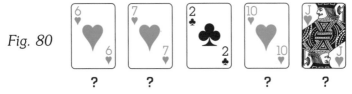

    ?   ?   ?   ?

The only comprehensive values that concern us here are the values of four of a Flush, including two, one or no Jacks and higher.

		4 OF A FLUSH
	Small cards	95¢
Table 32	One picture card	$1.02¢
	Two picture cards	$1.09¢

These values exceed all the Straight Flush values for three cards except the Ten Jack Queen which, of course, we have dealt with before and it is the Royal Flush possibility that gives the high values.

> When dealt four of a Flush, which includes three cards of a Straight Flush, always hold all four cards.

Let us picture the most juicy-looking hand, just to show you how seldom it seems that a Straight Flush is the viable option.

Fig. 81

HELD   HELD   HELD   HELD

STRAIGHT OR STRAIGHT FLUSH

We obviously would not be comparing three of a Straight to three of a Straight Flush. We want to know what option to take when a fourth card is in the same sequence of cards as three of the same suit.

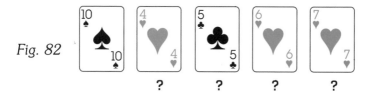

Fig. 82

?   ?   ?   ?

To be able to compare values, we must detail the values of drawing one card for a Straight. Again we have an *open* and *closed* Straight.

Table 33	OPEN	CLOSED
4 Small cards	68.1¢	34.0¢
including 1 Jack or higher	74.5¢	40.4¢
including 2 Jacks or higher	80.9¢	46.8¢

When comparing these values to those in Table 30, clear thinking must prevail. For instance, drawing for an *open* Straight may have to be compared to a *half open* Straight Flush option or an *open* one. The comparisons are combined in two tables :

73

Table 34

	4 OF OPEN STRAIGHT	3 OF OPEN STRAIGHT FLUSH	3 OF HALF-OPEN STRAIGHT FLUSH
4 small cards	68.1¢	59.7¢	50.0¢
incl. 1 Jack or higher	74.5¢	69.7¢	59.9¢
incl. 2 Jacks or higher	80.9¢	$/Flush	69.9¢

> When dealt four of an **Open Straight,** which includes three of a possible Straight Flush, always hold all four cards.

Table 35

	4 OF A CLOSED STRAIGHT	3 OF AN OPEN STRAIGHT FLUSH	3 OF HALF OPEN STRAIGHT FLUSH	3 OF CLOSED STRAIGHT FLUSH
4 small cards	34.0¢	59.7¢	50.0¢	40.0¢
incl. 1 Jack or higher	40.4¢	69.7¢	59.9¢	50.2¢
incl. 2 Jacks or higher	46.8¢	$ Flush	69.9¢	60.2¢.

All values work opposite to an **open** Straight.

> When dealt four of a **closed** Straight, which includes three of a possible Straight Flush, always go for the Straight Flush.

At this point, we need some graphics to illustrate the best values we have discovered.

Fig. 83

HELD HELD

Fig. 84

HELD HELD HELD HELD

Fig. 85

HELD   HELD   HELD

DIRECT COMPARATIVE OPTIONS

Up to now we have investigated whether or not to break up a Straight Flush option in favor of a better one. We now look at direct comparisons of choosing between two distinct options.

SMALL PAIR OR STRAIGHT FLUSH

The small pair could form part of the Straight Flush or stand on its own.

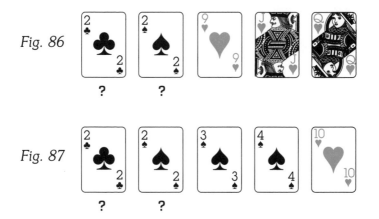

Fig. 86

Fig. 87

The value of a small pair is 79.3¢ and exceeds all the values of the Straight Flush options.

> Always hold a small pair in preference to any three cards of a Straight Flush.

75

It will thus go without saying that :

> Always hold a pair of Jacks and higher in prefer-
> ence to any three cards of a Straight Flush.

ONE PICTURE CARD vs STRAIGHT FLUSH

You will remember that we are comparing a picture card
separate to a three card Straight Flush option.

Fig. 88

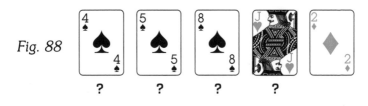

?   ?   ?   ?

CLOSED STRAIGHT FLUSH

We must revalue the option of a Straight Flush in view of
the fact that, by discarding a picture card, we lose the
chance of picking up a pair of Jacks or higher. The table
below tells the story :

	HOLDING	THREE CARD STRAIGHT FLUSH (DISCARDING 1 HONOR)	
Table 36	J 47.6¢	Open	59.4¢
	Q 47.0¢	Half open	49.7¢
	K 46.7¢	Closed	40.0¢
	A 46.4¢		

> Never hold a picture card in preference to any
> three card Straight Flush except a **closed** one.

In Fig. 88 you would hold the Jack.

Fig. 89

HELD   HELD   HELD

76

Fig. 90

HELD   HELD   HELD

TWO PICTURE CARDS vs STRAIGHT FLUSH

Fig. 91

We already know that two honor cards are valued better than one. Also, if we discard them, the value of the three Straight Flush cards diminishes.

Table 37

HOLDING	DIFFERENT SUITS	SAME SUITS	THREE CARD STRAIGHT FLUSH (DISCARDING 2 HONORS)	
J Q	50.9¢	62.6¢	Open	59.1¢
J K	49.7¢	61.2¢	Half open	49.4¢
J A	48.2¢	59.4¢	Closed	39.7¢
Q K	49.7¢	61.2¢		
Q A	48.2¢	59.4¢		
K A	48.2¢	59.4¢		
10 J	39.4¢	51.3¢		
10 Q	38.2¢	49.9¢		
10 K	37.0¢	48.4¢		
10 A	35.4¢	46.6¢		

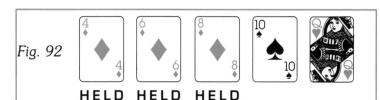

Fig. 92

HELD HELD HELD

Never hold a Ten of a different suit because it actually reduces the value of the honor. That is why the *closed* Straight Flush option is preferable but, of course, you should hold the following :

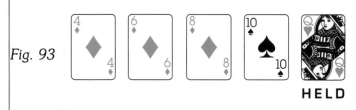

Fig. 93

HELD

I'm just starting to test you—wait for the Quiz!

Table 37 will result in the following rules:

> Always hold three cards of an **open** Straight Flush in preference to two picture cards of different suits.

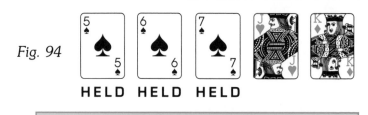

Fig. 94

HELD HELD HELD

> Never hold a **closed** Straight Flush in preference to two picture cards Always hold the picture cards.

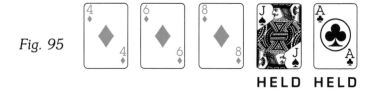

Fig. 95

HELD HELD

78

Now we must unravel the three card **half open** and **open** Straight Flushes.

> When dealt two cards of the Royal Flush which are three cards of a **closed** Straight Flush, always hold the pictures except when a Ten is part of the Royalty, then hold the Straight Flush cards.

EXAMPLES

Fig. 96

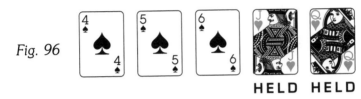

The advantage here is between 0.5% and 5.9% depending on which picture cards you hold.

Fig. 97

The advantage here is between 15.2% and 26.8%. The worst discards are the Ten and Ace.

> The Jack and Queen of different suits are **held** in favor of a **half open** three card Straight Flush, but are discarded in favor of an **open** one.

Fig. 98

Fig. 99

HELD   HELD   HELD

Lastly :

When dealt two honor cards of the same suit, including the Ten, hold them in favor of a **half open** three card Straight Flush except for the Ten King and Ten Ace.

When dealt three cards of an **open** Straight Flush and two picture cards of the **same suit**, always hold the picture cards.

Always hold an **open** three card Straight Flush in favor of the Ten and picture card of the same suit.

Fig. 100

HELD   HELD

Fig. 101

HELD   HELD   HELD

80

BARNES & NOBLE

STORE #2607 BURNSVILLE, MN 612-898-4509

REG#03   BOOKSELLER#026
RECEIPT#   3161 03/28/96   8:50 PM

CUSTOMER COPY

0806516054   WIN AT VIDEO POKER
              1 @   9.95   9.95

SUBTOTAL   9.95
SALES TAX - 6.5%   .65
TOTAL   10.60
VISA PAYMENT   10.60
ACCOUNT# 4190021190083533   EXP 1097
AUTHORIZATION# 041205   CLERK 26

BOOKSELLERS SINCE 1873

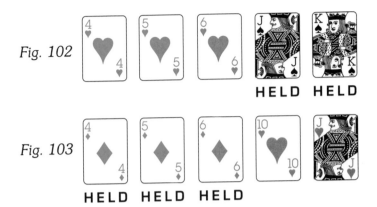

Fig. 102

Fig. 103

FOUR CARDS OF A STRAIGHT FLUSH

This decision making will be very straight forward and designed to reinforce some of the decisions that you have previously made.

The best four card Straight Flush that can be dealt to you is the following :

Fig. 104

This value is $3.51 because it is open ended and contains the maximum number of honors before it becomes Royal Flush material! The worst would be just the opposite, i.e. *closed* with no honors.

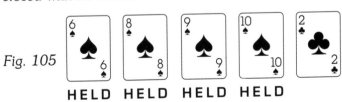

Fig. 105

This value is $2.17.

All we have to do is decide whether there is any situation which would warrant a decision.

Fig. 106

A pair of Jacks or higher only has a value of $1.51, so hold the Straight Flush cards.

The next two examples are the only other two that could concern you :

Fig. 107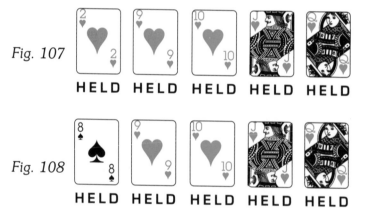

Above you have been dealt a Flush and a Straight. The Flush already has a value of $5.00 and the Straight $4.00, which exceeds the best potential of four cards of a Straight Flush.

> When dealt a Straight or a Flush which contains four cards of a Straight Flush, always hold all the cards.

This should complete the analysis of the Straight Flush and should put you in the *know* as to the best selections.

Just for the record, mention must be made of the sequence from Ace to Five:

The following are **closed:** A 2 3   A 2 3 4   A 2 4 5
These are **half open**   2 3 4   2 3 4 5

These observe the rules we have laid down in this chapter.

Few Straight Flushes are achieved, probably because the payout of 50 to 1 is far too low. This tends to make the most unlikely seeming potential wins more viable.

A few years ago I entered a Salon Privé to hear a Video Poker machine paying out its credits. Standing next to it was an overweight, gentleman looking as chuffed as a cat full of beer.

With pride and aggression he said: "I've just caught the *rare bitch*!" Unfortunate as the expression is, I have never forgotten it. It just seems to explain it all.

6 *PROGRESSIVE PLAY*

Up and up those numbers move! That tantalizing pot of gold just waiting for the next Royal Flush. This is surely what dreams are made of.

Outside of playing a high denomination machine, this is your chance to win a Royal Flush and a lot of money, for a low investment.

Luck can always be on your side. Royal Flushes can be dealt, even redealt after drawing one card. You will always have a degree of luck, but why not play scientifically as well? You then have both chances.

Every time you deal a hand there is a chance of a Royal Flush. After the first deal, your chance is a reality—or not. It does not depend on how many credits you have in a particular machine. Your Royal Flush will come to you when it's ready, you don't have to chase after it.

We now have to recognize every opportunity of exposing ourselves to drawing a Royal Flush, but not at the risk of wasting money.

The point here is that when the mathematics is in your favor, you should take the chance. The other option is best explained by the following example:

Fig. 109

The progressive jackpot is standing at $25,000 for five $1 coins. What cards are you going to hold? The temptation is to hold the 10 & J to at least have a chance of getting the Royal Flush. Imagine holding that combination 20,000 times. Your return would be $73,600 for every $100,000 against a higher return by holding the 10 J Q & K which would give a return of $87,200. An 18.5% increase in your return—and that takes the value of the Progressive Jackpot into account.

This chapter explores the changes in tactics you must make in your play as the Progressive Jackpot rises. You will take any winning opportunities and not waste any money. We'll leave luck out of it.

At the end of the chapter you will have a *barometer* to spare your memory and to use as a comparison, while wading through the theory. Some remarkable rules are going to unfold. There are situations where you may have to break up a winning hand to be better off in the long run. This may bring more more profit than taking risky long shot chances when you start with a lousy hand.

We are going to investigate every chance of drawing a Royal Flush and check what Progressive Jackpot value we will need to take that option.

We will always use the Progressive Jackpot value of a one Rand machine using **five coins**. We will quote the figures in real money. The maximum will be $25,000 which, barring a fluke, would not occur.

HOLDING ONE CARD OF THE ROYAL FLUSH

Fig. 110

Some players may feel that holding a ten is a good bet when the Progressive Jackpot is extremely high. Your first shock is the value of the single card against the Progressive Jackpot.

		PROGRESSIVE JACKPOT	
	HOLD	$5,000	$25,000
	10	$1.61	$1.72
	J	$2.38	$2.49
Table 38	Q	$2.35	$2.46
	K	$2.34	$2.44
	A	$2.32	$2.43

Notice, there is not much increase in value even against an extraordinarily high Progressive Jackpot. A small pair of $3.97 value is obviously a better option. Naturally a pair of Jacks or higher is even better to hold.

The case does not exist when one card of a Royal Flush is preferred to holding a pair.

> Never hold a one card of the Royal Flush in prefer-
> ence to a pair of Jacks or higher, or a small pair.

For academic reasons, the Progressive Jackpot would have to exceed $288,300 before you would drop a small pair for a Jack. Not likely on a R1 machine.

The rule has been that you hold two picture cards of different suits in preference to dropping one. As the table below shows, this rule still applies.

	DIFF SUITS		HOLDING ONE PICTURE CARD, DROPPING ANOTHER	
	JQ	50.9¢	J	48.2¢
Table 39	JK	49.7¢	Q	47.8¢
	JA	48.2¢	K	47.4¢
			A	47.2¢

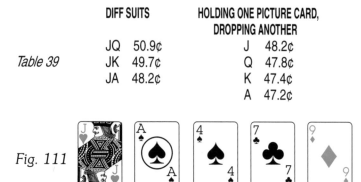

Fig. 111

HELD

It appears that the only two picture cards which should be split is Jack and Ace. Unfortunately this would only occur when the Progressive Jackpot exceeds $48,760

Fig. 112

When one of the Royal Flush forms part of a three card **straight flush**, the rules are the same as before—*go for the Straight Flush* under all circumstances. This must of course hold true for four of a straight flush and four of a flush.

Four cards of a straight containing one Royal card is valued at 74.5¢ for open and 40.4¢ for a closed one. The only open example has to contain the ten as well and will be dealt with later.

For a **closed** four card straight, observe the usual rule of holding the Royal card only.

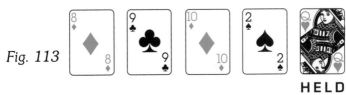

Fig. 113

HELD

CLOSED FOUR CARD STRAIGHT

A different situation occurs when a three card straight flush is **separate** to one picture card.

The table is calculated using a Royal Flush payout of $25,000

	HOLDING	THREE CARD STRAIGHT FLUSH	
	J 49.8¢	(DISCARDING ONE PICTURE CARD)	
Table 40	Q 49.2¢	Open	59.4¢
	K 48.9¢	Half open	49.7¢
	A 48.7¢	Closed	40.0¢

The only tactical change is to hold a Jack instead of a half open straight flush at $23,660. Otherwise all the rules are the same

Fig. 114

HELD

HOLDING TWO CARDS OF A ROYAL FLUSH

All through the book, when more than one Royal card has been held, the value has always been determined by the highest card. For easier reading, we will only use one combination to explain a situation, i.e. JA will replace JA, QA & KA as the values are the same.

The first point to consider is when two of the Royal Flush is a better option than holding a pair of Jacks or higher and a small pair.

The value of a Pair of Jacks stays static at $1.50 and a small pair at 79.3¢.

		PROGRESSIVE JACKPOT VALUE	
		$5,000	$25,000
	10J	39.4¢	46.1¢
	10Q	38.2¢	45.8¢
Table 41	10K	37.0¢	45.5¢
	10A	35.4¢	45.3¢

This table eliminates the question of *ever* holding a ten and picture card of the same suit in preference to any pair.

TWO PICTURE CARDS

Fig. 115

HELD   HELD

The values at some stage do exceed the value of a **small pair,** here are the Progressive Jackpot values.

		PROGRESSIVE JACKPOT (FOR DISCARDING A SMALL PAIR)
	JQ	$18,535
Table 42	QK, JK	$19,700
	QA, KA, JA	$21,185

The rule has been that when you are dealt the ten and two picture cards, one the same suit as the ten, that you never hold all three.

The following is the list of thresholds for holding the 10 and a picture card in preference to the same picture card and the one being discarded.

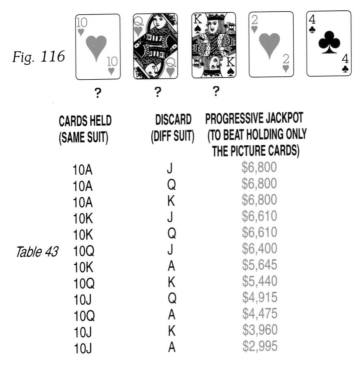

Fig. 116

CARDS HELD (SAME SUIT)	DISCARD (DIFF SUIT)	PROGRESSIVE JACKPOT (TO BEAT HOLDING ONLY THE PICTURE CARDS)
10A	J	$6,800
10A	Q	$6,800
10A	K	$6,800
10K	J	$6,610
10K	Q	$6,610
10Q	J	$6,400
10K	A	$5,645
10Q	K	$5,440
10J	Q	$4,915
10Q	A	$4,475
10J	K	$3,960
10J	A	$2,995

Table 43

This means that until the Jackpot reaches the figure above, the better option is to hold the picture cards.

There are Video Poker machines which are set to pay back 100% or more. The casino is reliant on the players' error factor to make a profit.

TWO ROYALTY OF SAME SUIT AND DISCARDING TWO

The following list of thresholds shows the jackpot value in holding the two royalty of the same suit and discarding the other two. The option must be superior to potential straights.

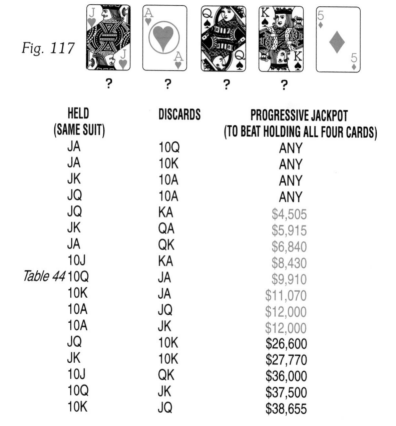

Fig. 117

HELD (SAME SUIT)	DISCARDS	PROGRESSIVE JACKPOT (TO BEAT HOLDING ALL FOUR CARDS)
JA	10Q	ANY
JA	10K	ANY
JK	10A	ANY
JQ	10A	ANY
JQ	KA	$4,505
JK	QA	$5,915
JA	QK	$6,840
10J	KA	$8,430
10Q	JA	$9,910
10K	JA	$11,070
10A	JQ	$12,000
10A	JK	$12,000
JQ	10K	$26,600
JK	10K	$27,770
10J	QK	$36,000
10Q	JK	$37,500
10K	JQ	$38,655

Table 44

If the above seems confusing, the reason is that there is always a time to hold for the Royal Flush but it must beat any other options available. In the above case the option had to be better than drawing for a Straight. viz. 4 of the Straight.

Jack to Ace	59.6¢
Ten to Ace	53.2¢
Ten to King	87.2¢

All the 10 to King straights need Progressive Jackpots too high to break up so hold all four cards and *go for the straight.*

There is another special case we must not forget about. What should your strategy be if a pair of tens was included in your cards drawn?

Fig. 118

HELD HELD

	HELD CARDS	DISCARDS	PROGRESSIVE JACKPOT (TO BEAT HOLDING A PAIR OF TENS)
	JQ	10,10A	$20,200
	JK	10,10A	$21,360
	JA	10,10Q	$22,290
	JA	10,10K	$22,290
Table 45	10J	10KA	$29,600
	10Q	10JA	$31,085
	10K	10JA	$32,245
	10A	10JQ	$33,175
	10A	10JK	$33,175

Always hold the pair of tens unless the selection chosen exceeds the Progressive Jackpot above. You will also realize that with two tens, you would often be able to choose which of two suits to group. In all cases, however, the Progressive Jackpot would have to be too high.

It is very common that you have only two suits in the four cards dealt. From the above you will be able to choose which is the better pair of the two to hold.

92

TWO ROYALTY VERSUS 3 OF STRAIGHT FLUSH

(A) TWO ROYALTY INCLUDED IN 3 OF STRAIGHT FLUSH

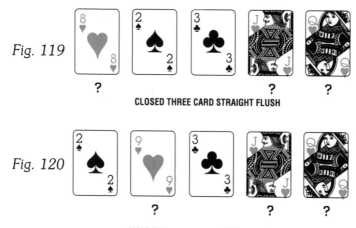

Fig. 119

?   ?   ?

CLOSED THREE CARD STRAIGHT FLUSH

Fig. 120

?   ?   ?

HALF OPEN THREE CARD STRAIGHT FLUSH

	PROGRESSIVE JACKPOT TO HOLD ONLY THE TWO ROYALTY CARDS	
HELD	CLOSED STRAIGHT FLUSH	HALF OPEN S/F
JQ	$4,380	$12,260
JK	$5,860	$13,740
Table 46 QK	$5,860	$13,740
10J	$13,960	$21,750
10Q	$14,835	$22,720
10K	$16,200	$24,080

The Progressive Jackpot must reach the above levels before you hold only the pair of Royalty. The only **open** 3 card straight flush with two Royalty must have the Ten as the third card and you will always hold all three.

B) TWO ROYALTY SEPARATE FROM 3 OF STRAIGHT FLUSH

Fig. 121

Fig. 122

OPEN THREE CARD STRAIGHT FLUSH

		PROGRESSIVE JACKPOT TO HOLD THE ROYALTY	
HELD	**CLOSED S/F**	**HALF OPEN S/F**	**OPEN S/F**
JQ	0	0	$2,150
JK, QK	0	0	$3,315
JA, QA, KA	0	$3,070	$4,800
Table 47 10J	0	$3,445	$11,320
10Q	0	$4,615	$12,485
10K	0	$5,775	$13,645
10A	0	$7,265	$15,140

The zeros stand for any value of Royal Flush Jackpot.

HOLDING 3 ROYALTY OF THE SAME SUIT

Fig. 123

HELD   HELD   HELD

You already know that when you are dealt four Royalty of which three are of the same suit, you never draw for a straight. You always hold the three Royalty.

We are then left with assessing at what Progressive Jackpot value we hold the three Royalty in preference to other options.

Fig. 124

?   ?   ?

94

THREE ROYALTY VERSUS PAIR JACKS OR HIGHER

	HOLD	PROGRESSIVE JACKPOT (TO DISCARD A PAIR OF JACKS OR HIGHER)
	JQK	$4,170
	10JQ	$4,260
	JQA	$4,690
	JKA	$4,690
	QKA	$4,690
Table 48	10JK	$4,785
	10QK	$4,785
	10JA	$5,230
	10QA	$5,230
	10KA	$5,230

In the past, only you know whether you have ever contemplated discarding a pair of Jacks and higher. So much for the saying that you never break up a winning hand. These Progressive Jackpot levels are quite realistic so your style of play is going to change.

THREE ROYALTY VERSUS TWO PAIRS

Fig. 125

This is another quite attainable situation. Players who play in *automatic mode* and just automatically hold winning combinations may miss Royal Flush opportunities by not checking carefully before selecting cards.

HOLD	PROGRESSIVE JACKPOT (TO DISCARD TWO PAIRS)
JQK	$8,680
10JQ	$8,770
JQA	$9,190
JKA	$9,190
QKA	$9,190
10JK	$9,295
10QK	$9,295
10JA	$9,740
10QA	$9,740
10KA	$9,740

Table 49 is to the left of the QKA row.

THREE ROYALTY VERSUS 3 OF A KIND

Fig. 126

? ? ?

If you didn't think this situation was possible, here is an example. If you thought that there was anything better than holding the trip, here is the list of Progressive Jackpot values at which point you would break up the trip in favor of a shot at the Royal Flush, believe it or not.

HELD	PROGRESSIVE JACKPOT (TO DISCARD THE TRIP)
JQK	$18,295
10JQ	$18,385
JQA	$18,810
JKA	$18,810
QKA	$18,810
10JK	$18,910
10QK	$18,910
10JA	$19,355
10QA	$19,355
10KA	$19,355

Table 50 is to the left of the 10JK row.

Very high jackpots are surely worth a certain risk at a point. The points are there. Do not break up the combinations before the jackpot has reached these levels. That will be wasting your money. Above these levels, the mathematics favor you.

THREE ROYALTY VERSUS DEALT STRAIGHT

Fig. 127

? ? ?

Although these situations will not often crop up, its better to know where you stand

HELD	PROGRESSIVE JACKPOT (TO BREAK UP A DEALT STRAIGHT)
JQK	$17,785
10JQ	$17,815
JQA	$18,230
JKA	$18,230
QKA	$18,230
10JK	$18,340
10QK	$18,340
10JA	$18,785
10QA	$18,785
10KA	$18,785

Table 51

These values are lower than breaking up a trip.
This is explained by a trip bring worth $4.12 in the long run against the straight being held at $4.00.

THREE ROYALTY VERSUS A DEALT FLUSH

Fig. 128

While we are at it, let us see whether this falls into our scope of the book of falling under a Progressive Jackpot of $25,000 for five $1 coins.

97

HELD	PROGRESSIVE JACKPOT (TO BREAK A DEALT FLUSH)
JQK	$23,380
10JQ	$23,595
JQA	$24,105
JKA	$24,105
QKA	$24,105
10JK	$24,120
10QK	$24,120
10JA	$24,650
10QA	$24,650
10KA	$24,650

Table 52

ANOTHER SPECIAL CASE

Would you break up a dealt straight flush like this?

Fig. 129

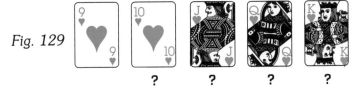

? ? ? ?

Mathematically as long as the Progressive Jackpot exceeds $11,410, it pays you to drop the nine of hearts.

When the progressive jackpot of a 6/5 Video Poker machine reaches $16,500, it is actually in your favor.

	CARDS HELD OF SAME SUIT	DISCARDS OR BREAK-UP
24 650	10JA, 10QA, 10KA	Flush
24 120	10JK, 10QK	Flush
24 105	JKA, QKA	Flush
24 080	10K	Part of Half Open S/F
23 600	J	Part of Half Open S/F
23 595	10JQ	Flush
23 380	JQK	Flush
22 720	10Q	Part of Half Open S/F
22 290	JA	10,10 Q or K of Different Suits
21 750	10J	Part of Half Open S/F
21 360	JK	10,10 A of Different Suits
21 185	JA, QA, KA	Small pair
20 200	JQ	10, 10A of Different Suits
19 700	JK, QK	Small pair
19 355	10JA, 10QA, 10KA	Trip
18 910	10JK, 10QK	Trip
18 810	JQA, JKA, QKA	Trip
18 775	10JA, 10QA, 10KA	Straight
18 535	JQ	Small pair
18 385	10JQ	Trip
18 340	10JK, 10QK	Straight
18 295	JQK	Trip
18 230	JQA, JKA, QKA	Straight
17 815	10JQ	Straight
17 785	JQK	Straight
16 200	10K	Part of Closed S/F
15 140	10A	Sep 3 of Open S/F
14 835	10Q	Part of Closed S/F
13 960	10J	Part of Closed S/F
13 740	JK, QK	Part of Half Open S/F
13 645	10K	Sep 3 of Open S/F
12 485	10Q	Sep 3 of Open S/F
12 260	JQ	Part of Half Open S/F
12 000	10A	JQ or JK of Different Suits
11 410	10JQK	9 of Same Suit
11 320	10J	Sep 3 of Open S/F
11 070	10K	JA of Different Suits
9 910	10Q	JA of Different Suits
9 740	10JA, 10QA, 10KA	2 pairs
9 295	10JK, 10QK	2 pairs
9 190	JQA, JKA, QKA	2 pairs
8 770	10JQ	2 pairs
8 680	JQK	2 pairs
8 430	10J	KA of Different Suits
7 265	10A	Sep 3 of Half Open S/F
6 840	JA	QK of Different Suits
6 800	10A	J, Q or K of Different Suits
6 610	10K	J or Q of Different Suits
6 400	10Q	J of Different Suits
5 915	JK	QA of Different Suits
5 860	JK, QK	Part of Closed S/F
5 775	10K	Sep 3 of Half Open S/F
5 645	10K	A of Different Suit
5 440	10Q	K of Different Suit
5 230	10JA, 10QA, 10KA	Pair Jacks or Higher
4 915	10J	Q of Different Suit
4 800	JA, QA, KA	Sep 3 of Open S/F
4 615	10Q	Sep 3 of Half Open S/F
4 505	JQ	KA of Different Suits
4 475	10Q	A of Different Suit
4 380	JQ	Part of Closed S/F

PROGRESSIVE JACKPOT

When the Progressive Jackpot exceeds any of the figures featured in the Barometer, take the new options and any below it.

7 TACTICAL CHANGES

We all know that the payout scales of Video Poker machines vary. Apart from providing screen variety, the differences are based on low and high denominations.

You may have personal reasons for playing a particular machine, but always check the payout scale to ascertain what changes in card selection you will need to adopt.

This section assumes that you are fully acquainted with the book so far. My assumptions up to this point were based on a payout scale paying 6 for a Full House and 5 for a Flush (called a 6/5 machine). For simplicity I'll only mention selections that will differ from what you've learned already.

It's just as important to know when no change in selection is necessary. This reassurance will be helpful as one can be blinded by higher payouts, which lead a player to take unnecessary risks.

And remember—all advice is based on playing the maximum number of coins to enjoy the highest payouts available.

THE 8/5 VIDEO POKER MACHINE

The payout scale of this machine is as follows:

	1 COIN	5 COINS
Royal Flush	250	5,000
Straight Flush	50	250
4 of a Kind	25	125
Full House	8	40
Flush	5	25
Straight	4	20
3 of a Kind	3	15
2 Pairs	2	10
Pr Jacks or Higher	1	5

Whenever you achieve a Full House you will receive $10 more on this machine. In most sessions of play you'll get this a couple of times.

Strangely there are very few selection changes. Every two card selection only increases about 0.4¢ because of the influence of the Full House payout.

The only change in values that concerns us is a small pair which is now valued at 81.4¢ and the open 4 card straight including two picture cards which remains at 80.9¢. Out of these there are actually only two possibilities and they are pictured below:

Fig. 130

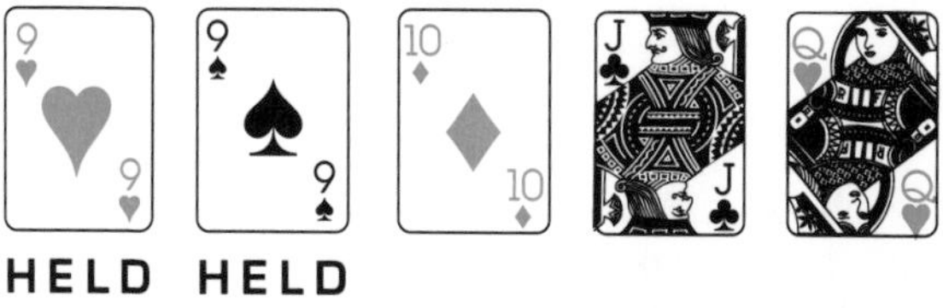

HELD   HELD

Fig. 131

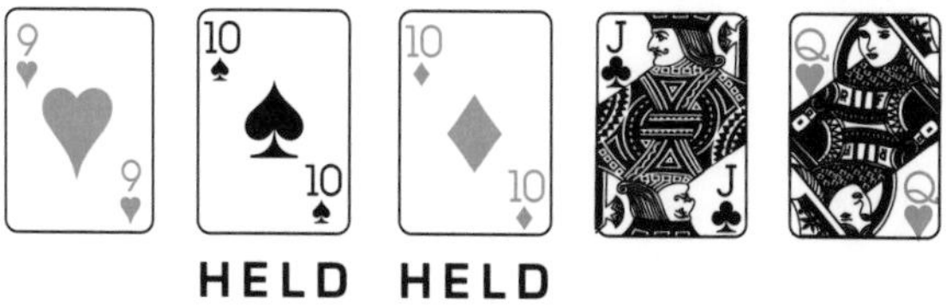

HELD   HELD

THE 8/5 VIDEO POKER MACHINE WITH 100 STRAIGHT FLUSH PAYOUT

	1 COIN	5 COINS
Royal Flush	500	4,000
Straight Flush	100	500
4 of a kind	25	125
Full House	8	40
Flush	5	25
Straight	4	20
3 of a kind	3	15
2 pairs	2	10
Pair Jacks and higher	1	5

This machine is distinguished by the way it unfolds the cards on the screen. It seems to imitate the unfolding of real cards and plays a tune to alert that you have a winning hand.

Another feature is that the machine **automatically holds** any winning combinations. In addition, it will always hold a small pair and this can cause a problem; as many times this is not the best option.

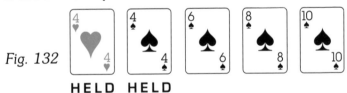

Fig. 132

HELD   HELD

WRONG SELECTION!

In the above example, the best option is actually to hold the spades and *go for a flush*. Simply press the buttons to deselect the combination and hold the cards of your choice.

Other winning combinations will be held automatically so check first before you proceed.

102

Below are some other dealt hands for which to watch out:

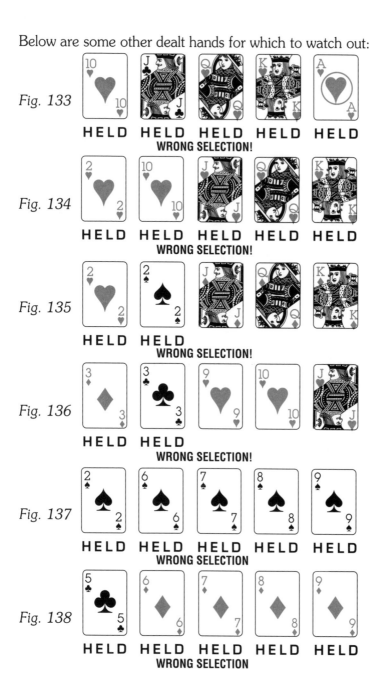

Fig. 133

HELD HELD HELD HELD HELD
WRONG SELECTION!

Fig. 134

HELD HELD HELD HELD HELD
WRONG SELECTION!

Fig. 135

HELD HELD
WRONG SELECTION!

Fig. 136

HELD HELD
WRONG SELECTION!

Fig. 137

HELD HELD HELD HELD HELD
WRONG SELECTION

Fig. 138

HELD HELD HELD HELD HELD
WRONG SELECTION

103

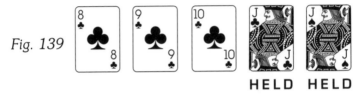

Fig. 139

HELD HELD

WRONG SELECTION!

FULL HOUSE DIFFERENCE

Some versions of this machine pay out 6 for 1 for a Full House and the rest 8 for 1. Obviously the 8 payout is worth more to play but tactically there are very few differences. Let us just picture the differences when playing the 8 Full House instead of the 6.

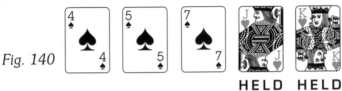

Fig. 140

HELD HELD

HALF OPEN STRAIGHT FLUSH

Specifically the King must be one of the two picture cards of the same suit that takes preference over a three card half open Straight flush.

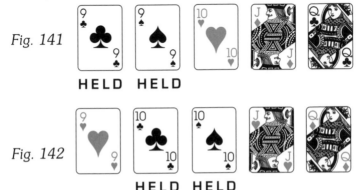

Fig. 141

HELD HELD

Fig. 142

HELD HELD

The above two hands are the only other two examples of

holding a small pair in preference to an open straight flush containing two picture cards.

In other words you must reverse these selections when playing the 6 for 1 full house machine.

SELECTION CHANGES

With the Straight Flush paying out double the normal, it does not double the value of holding a selection which exposes you to the possibility. The reason is because the value of a held hand will include all the other wins you may qualify for, i.e. Pairs, Jacks and higher, two pairs, trip, straight, flush.

A few examples to illustrate this point are:

CARDS HELD	STRAIGHT FLUSH AT 50 FOR 1	STRAIGHT FLUSH AT 100 FOR 1
4,5,6, same suit	59.7¢	73.5¢
9,10,J same suit	69.7¢	83.5¢
10,J,Q same suit	$1.68	$1.77
6,8,9,10 same suit	$2.17	$3.23
9,10,J,Q same suit	$3.51	$5.64

The closer you are to the Straight flush the wider the margin becomes.

For the first time an Open Straight Flush beats an Open Straight.

Fig. 143

HELD   HELD   HELD

Fig. 144

The second example does not work when you discard the Jack.

Fig. 145

OPEN STRAIGHT AND OPEN STRAIGHT FLUSH INCLUDING ONE JACK OR HIGHER

The Small Pair is not held as usual in the case of a Closed Straight Flush including one Jack or higher.

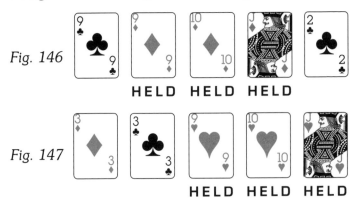

Fig. 146

Fig. 147

All Open and Half Open straight flushes take preference over two picture cards of different suits.

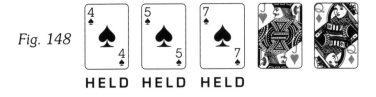

Fig. 148

THREE CARD HALF OPEN STRAIGHT FLUSH

Fig. 149

HELD   HELD   HELD

THREE CARD OPEN STRAIGHT FLUSH

All Open Straight Flushes take preference over two Royalty Cards.

Fig. 150

HELD   HELD   HELD

Here are two more hands that work in an opposite way to other machines; that is breaking up a winning flush or straight that contains four cards of an Open Straight Flush, not a closed one.

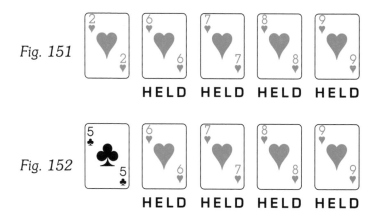

Fig. 151

HELD   HELD   HELD   HELD

Fig. 152

HELD   HELD   HELD   HELD

107

THE 9/6 VIDEO POKER MACHINE

This machine has the highest basic payout scale. It's undoubtedly the most profitable one to play. Unfortunately, it's usually associated with a high denomination coin. If you are nervous about playing so much money it may make you fail to spot the best selection options in favor of a dealt win. This is self-defeating so play the 9/6 machine only when you can afford to play it properly.

	1 COIN	5 COINS
Royal Flush	250	5,000
Straight Flush	50	250
4 of a kind	25	125
Full House	9	45
Flush	6	30
Straight	4	20
3 of a Kind	3	15
Two Pairs	2	10
Pr Jacks or Higher	1	5

Again just the variations from the norm are detailed below with some memory prompts to help.

Fig. 153

HELD HELD

It was only the Ten and Jack you held, but now it is the Ten and Queen as well.

Fig. 154

HELD HELD

This is specifically in this case when the Ace is included.

Fig. 155

HELD   HELD

This is in preference to holding all four and includes JK and JQ.

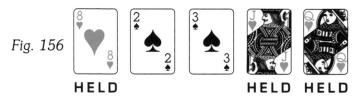

Fig. 156

HELD   HELD   HELD

POTENTIAL CLOSED STRAIGHT FLUSH

This example is now included in addition to the existing 9JK, 9QK. Remember half open and open Straight Flushes are already held because they have a higher value.

Fig. 157

HELD   HELD   HELD

POTENTIAL HALF OPEN STRAIGHT FLUSH

This reverses the previous option and now includes holding against all pairs of Royalty of different suits.

Fig. 158

HELD   HELD   HELD

POTENTIAL OPEN STRAIGHT FLUSH

109

This holds for all pairs of Royalty except specifically the Jack and Queen (as before).

Fig. 159

HELD   HELD   HELD

POTENTIAL HALF OPEN STRAIGHT FLUSH

The Half Open Straight Flush now is the better option against all royalty including the Ten.

This section on Tactical Changes has been based on having a full knowledge of Chapters three, four and five. You have to know the basic rules or else you will only confuse yourself by looking at the changes in isolation.

Where you may have a problem memorizing the rules immediately, try to understand the basic principles that are involved. For argument's sake: if a closed Straight Flush is the option to hold in this section, it stands to reason that a Half Open or Open will do just as well.

To save space I have detailed only the exceptions. When we discuss Bonus machines and specific reference is not made to holding, say, an Ace, then it has no particular relevance or advantage. We cannot detail every option not to take but rather the ones you must take.

Keep going . . . you have got this far and you must be doing well!

THE BONUS 4 OF A KIND VIDEO POKER MACHINE

	1 COIN	5 COINS
Royal Flush	250	4,000
4 of a Kind ACES	80	400
Straight Flush	50	250
4 of a Kind 2, 3, 4	40	200
Full House	8	40
Flush	5	30
Straight	4	20
3 of a Kind	3	15
Two Pairs	2	10
Pr Jacks or Higher	1	5

This is an extremely popular machine. Sometimes it's hard to get a seat at one. The bonus dream captures the imagination; there is something special about Penalty Aces. Here you get a payout more than three times the norm.

There are three forces acting to change the value of your selections. A selection can be lowered by the Royal Flush paying out 800 instead of 1,000. Then there is an increase in the Full House and the Aces, twos, threes and fours.

Again, all the original selection rules still stand except for the examples that will be detailed below. If this is a favorite machine of yours, try and memorize the new selections you will now make.

Fig. 160

HELD

No change in holding 10J, 10Q and 10K.

Fig. 161

HELD HELD

Still discard an Ace when dealt three picture cards.

Fig. 162

HELD HELD

The rule was to always hold the three royalty except when the Ace was involved. Now, in all cases, hold the pair of Jacks or higher.

Fig. 163

HELD HELD

Always hold the two picture cards except with the Ten and Jack of the same suit—discard the King or Ace!

Fig. 164

HELD HELD HELD HELD

Previously you would just hold the Jack and Queen of the same suit. In all cases hold all four cards.

Fig. 165

HELD   HELD HELD

POTENTIAL CLOSED STRAIGHT FLUSH

112

With two picture cards out of three in the potential closed Straight Flush always go for the Straight Flush.

Fig. 166

HELD HELD

POTENTIAL OPEN STRAIGHT FLUSH

This change is also true for QA and KA.

Fig. 167

HELD HELD

POTENTIAL HALF OPEN STRAIGHT FLUSH

The above already held for the 10J as well.

Let me remind you that when a Closed Straight Flush is the selection to take, this must also include the Half Open and Open because they increase in value.

Similarly if a selection works for the Jack and Ace of the same suit, it must also work if the higher of the two cards is a King or Queen.

Lastly, do not flatter the value of holding an Ace on its own. Holding either JA, QA or KA is worth 58.9¢. Holding just the Ace and discarding the other is worth 46.5¢. That's a disadvantage of 21%.

> Some Bonus machines pay 6 for a Full House. A Full House with three Aces is worth $6.00, but three Aces alone are worth $6.52, so discard the pair.

113

THE SELECT A BONUS 4 OF A KIND VIDEO POKER MACHINE

This machine adds some variety to Video Poker. The payout scale is as follows:

	1 COIN	5 COINS
Royal Flush	250	4,000
Straight Flush	50	250
4 Aces or a card of your choice	80	400
4 of a Kind	25	125
Full House	7	35
Flush	5	25
Straight	4	20
3 of a kind	3	15
Two Pairs	2	10
Pair of Jacks or Higher	1	5

This is a 7/5 machine which pays 80 coins for 4 Aces or for 4 of a card which you select. Which card to select is hard to suggest.

It's hard to suggest which card to select, but it's probably better to select a Jack, Queen or King. You have probably achieved penalties while holding one card so you may as well give yourself a chance. After all, there is never a reason to hold any one card between Two and Ten on it's own.

To select the card you want as the bonus one, simply press the **hold** button repeatedly before you play until the name appears on the screen.

The rules are the same as for the Bonus 4 of a Kind machine.

If your selected card is Ten or below, never hold it on its own as a redeal is worth more.

A joker's wild machine gives you a little edge. (Courtesy Casino Player, *the magazine for gaming enthusiasts.*)

8 COMPETITIONS & BUY-INS

COMPETITIONS

One Video Poker innovation has opened the door to a whole new dimension of excitement. I'm referring to machines which can be set for Tournament Play. Playing the same machines, we can now compete against fellow players in a genuine competition environment.

Many competitions are now held to find champions in different categories and regions. It is only a matter of time before we have a world champion. Wishful thinking would even have it as an Olympic Sport.

Like any other competition, Video Poker tournaments are full of tensions. The emotional roller-coaster swings from elation to disappointment. Skill, experience and practice are important ingredients, as in any other sport.

MACHINE SETTINGS

The Tournament Play setting of the machine is shown in the photo of the video screen. The left control is a timer which is activated the moment the first hand is dealt by you. It is preset in minutes and seconds and counts down to zero. The moment it zeros, the machine switches off on completion of the hand in progress. The timer can be set to any number of minutes. A popular interval of ten minutes is used in all our examples and references to time.

The middle meter records your score.

Every winning score is added on this meter. It is totally independent to the credit meter on the right. The meter rises with wins and does not decrease as credits are consumed to play a hand.

The meter on the right is again preset with the credits you can use in the time allocated for the session of play. It is usually set on a figure far in excess of the amount that can be used up in the time allowed. Some machines do not have this meter displayed on the Video screen. The setting simply allows you an inexhaustible number of credits to use.

Coins are not inserted into the machine and it operates completely electronically. Beside any initial cost of entering a competition, it is like playing Video Poker free of charge.

To activate each deal of cards and the start of the game, simply press either the Maximum Credits or Deal/Draw buttons. Hold the desired cards and press Deal/Draw to get your replacement cards. Any win will *almost* instantly be recorded on the win meter. It is thus possible to only use the Deal/Draw button the whole time to draw the initial deal and the redeal.

STYLES OF PLAY

It becomes clear very quickly that speed of play is a vital ingredient to success.

It can be very deceptive to watch people playing and assess their speed. Some appear much faster than others, but this is not always the case.

All fast players use both hands to minimize the distance the hands must travel around the controls. The first style we will call the *slapping* technique. This is very physical and fast and looks extremely dramatic. The controls take quite

117

a bashing but using this method does attain very fast play.

The other style we call the *piano* or typewriter technique. The fingers glide over the control buttons very much like those of a pianist or typist. It is not spectacular to watch but the speed of play can equal the first technique.

There is no style that has more of an advantage over the other. What does happen, however, is that the slappers do quiet down after a while, and achieve a slightly faster speed. Pick the style that most suits your fingers or hands and makes you feel most comfortable. Practice until the mechanical operations are instinctive and allow for the maximum concentration for card selection and speed.

Very good speeds consume 1,070 credits, at five a time, in ten minutes. That means one hand played completely every 2.8 seconds. Any speed around three seconds is good.

BASIC TACTICS

Already mentioned, speed of play is half the skill required. The other half is the card selection. The two skills intertwine in that some selections involve holding many cards. The split seconds lost in holding these cards can cancel out, or even reduce, an advantage over a more simple card selection. Only you will find the happy medium for yourself.

The average scores in a ten-minute session are between 850 and 1,050. This can vary when the speed of the machines is set slower or faster than normal.

The reason I mention this is to put the value of the winning combinations you achieve into perspective. Obviously, if you average a point for every credit used, you should score around 1,000 points.

118

This brings into focus the super scores that you wish on yourself during play. There are Penalties (125), Straight Flush (25) and Royal Flush (4,000). Achieving any one or two of these in a session would normally put you in a very strong position.

The highest score in a recent competition, which involved about 1,000 plays in practice and heats, was 1,405. This score included one Straight Flush and one Penalty. When someone achieved a Royal Flush, their score would have been about 5,000. *The most important card selection tactic is based on this very fact.*

First of all, Royal Flushes will be achieved about every 400 to 500 sessions of play. A very long shot in anyone's language. To rely on this to win competitions would leave you winning very few.

If you downgrade the value of the Royal Flush to 500 points (i.e. 100 for 1), two factors come into play. Firstly, you would not need its value more than 500 to win. Secondly, all the best selections and calculations are based on a Royal Flush paying 1,000 for 1. This means that every time you select cards that give the Royal Flush opportunity, an investment is made toward it.

Let us illustrate this by listing a selection of values based on a Royal Flush paying 100 and 1,000.

CARDS HELD	ROYAL FLUSH 100	ROYAL FLUSH 1 000
JQ	57.1¢	62.6¢
JK	55.6¢	61.2¢
QA	53.8¢	59.4¢
10J	45.8¢	51.3¢
10A	41.1¢	46.6¢

In each case 5.5 cents is the difference between the two values of the Royal Flush. That constitutes an investment of over 10% in the Royal Flush.

The problem here is that you may make some selections in preference to others based on the normal value of the Royal Flush. Other selections will give you a higher score in the short term. Many times the usual selection will be made because based on the reduced Royal Flush value, it may still be the best option. You will still be in the queue for the Royal Flush, as remote as it may be.

It is very important that if you are going to adopt these tactics, and follow the card selection differences that follow, you treat the Royal Flush merely as a Super Straight Flush. You now understand that to get one will win the round without the need to *pulverize* your fellow competitors.

CARD SELECTION

In Competition Play you have to adopt a slightly different strategy of card selection. A different emphasis is put on selection; it's simplicity in identifying at speed and the short term value that count.

Wayout selections and trying your luck will not work in the end. Most competitions are played over multiple rounds and the lucky player will be found out. The more rounds played, the more your skill will come to the fore.

Under the pressure and the need to minimize the loss of split seconds, the best selections are detailed roughly in order. You must immediately scan the payout scale, if it lights up for any initial hand-dealt win, hold the cards and *immediately* redeal.

The next are the myriad potential winning hands dealt. If you have the quick eye and hand speed for it, then look out for at least three of a Closed Straight Flush, four of a Flush or four of an open Straight.

120

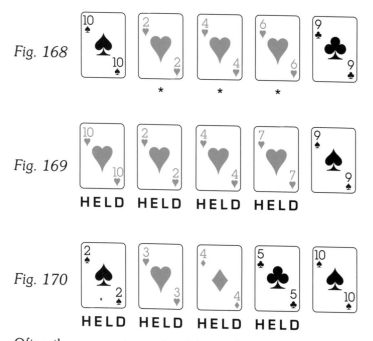

Fig. 168

Fig. 169

HELD   HELD   HELD   HELD

Fig. 170

HELD   HELD   HELD   HELD

Often they are not easy to pick out, but looking for them is a skill to acquire. This will put you in line, at least, to achieve a Straight Flush.

Definitely the next to look for, even before picture cards, are small pairs. Their value of 80¢ exceeds many three Royalty values.

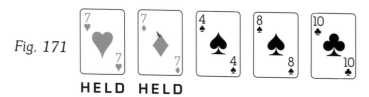

Fig. 171

HELD   HELD

As luck will have it, small pairs seem to hide away and one often misses seeing them. Other times they seem to stand out waiting to be held.

121

The next is to recognize which picture cards to hold. I mention picture cards because you should never hold a Ten with a one picture card, even of the same suit. That's a rule change for Tournament Play.

Fig. 172

HELD

Only hold a Ten of the same suit with at least two picture cards of the same suit, preferably four. This has the value of the Super Straight Flush, Straight Flush, Flush or Straight, which are good wins to get.

The same rule applies for value and speed when dealt three picture cards of different suits. If the Ace is included, *do not hold it!*

Fig. 173

HELD   HELD

Again when dealt three picture cards including two of the same suit, always discard the odd suit. This is a Royal Flush opportunity.

Fig. 174

HELD   HELD

Other examples of preferences in selection are pictured for reassurance and for you to memorize, so as to eventually select by instinct in a competition.

Fig. 175

HELD   HELD   HELD

Any *three card* Straight Flush is better than a *two card* Royal Flush opportunity.

Fig. 176

HELD   HELD

The small pair is still the better option. It goes to show that you will achieve Penalties, Full Houses or less far more often than Straight Flushes and Flushes. All in all, continuous small wins combined with the odd big win will put you ahead in any competition.

OTHER ADVICE

No matter how pressurized the competition makes you feel, always play sober. You may feel good after a drink but you'll will never know what could have been, thanks to missed selections and slower play.

When some comperes get the session going on a Ready, Set, Go basis, ignore it. You do not have to start on time. Wait until you are ready and start in your own time. You will not lose any time as all the machines work independently. Another advantage is that when interim scores are announced during the session, you know the others' scores and they do not know you still have more time than them.

You play poker to achieve winning combinations and it is very satisfying to admire a winning hand. Without realizing this, you have always done this. Another habit is to watch, with anticipation, as you are dealt 'Three of a Kind' and are drawing for Penalties or a Full House.

You must get rid of these two habits. Precious time is lost and for all practical purposes, it makes absolutely no difference what happens. Avoid studying the screen once you have held your cards; concentrate on redealing and dealing again in the shortest possible time.

The control buttons are not switches. When depressed they make *one* contact. Keeping your finger on them will not alter the initial contact that was made. While the meter on the machine is recording your score *nearly instantly*, the deal button is deactivated. When you press the button at this moment, nothing happens. You have to press the button *again* as holding it continually will not deal your cards. Since you don't know the split second that the deal button is alive again, get into the habit of pressing the deal button repeatedly to make sure you get the earliest deal. Your chance of redealing in error is remote as the machine takes a while to actually expose the cards.

In any ten minute session there will be a minute or two when your machine just does not seem to produce any winning combinations. This is a very vital juncture. You have to believe that it is only temporary and that it will soon change. Play faster and do not become disillusioned. The game's not over until you have played up to the very last second. The number of times that players have got Penalties at the last moment is amazing.

In *multiple heat* competitions, where your scores accumulate, it is even more important to remember this. Most of the time you will get a dead machine in one round. Do not slow down but rather try to extract every win you can. Remember five points in a bad round is just as valuable as in a good one. The same goes when you just know that you are accumulating a good score. Do not sit on your laurels and become casual. Your next round may be a dog.

The fact that you are not inserting coins but only playing for credits may take your *playing for free* too far. Do not play recklessly.

124

Competitions are great fun and develop a great vibe among the competitors, especially when the competition runs over a period of time, including heats, semi-finals and finals.

It does pay to enter them because the organizers always add extra cash to the pool of entrance fee money. Extra incentives and freebees are common and the general idea is having fun.

BUY-INS

This is the name given to instant competitions where the entrants all pay in a set amount and the winner takes the pool. Seldom are they played over more than one round so luck can play a more important part.

Even the less-skilled player, from a speed point of view, has as good a chance as any. Enter buy-ins whenever possible as it is good practice and the organizers always add extras to the cash pool.

Your strategy of card selection may be normal or with a few adaptations for speed purposes.

If, from an announcement over the PA system, you realise that you are lagging badly behind the leader, that may be the prompt to take *longer shot* selections.

All the calculations in this book are based on the best options *in the long run*. Here you have a mighty short run of only ten minutes. Anything can actually happen. No one ever said you cannot achieve a Straight Flush by holding only one card.

With the winner taking all, coming second does not count at all, so when you are badly behind take your chances with longer shots. In one quarter-final heat I was eighty in the lead with ten seconds to go and was beaten by over a hundred points. Point proved?

DOUBLING
& GAMBLING

Most Video Poker Machines will offer you the opportunity to double your money after a win. You may double as many times as you wish until you either claim your win or lose.

Many players are skeptical of this offer. They must be of the school of thought that the casino never offers you anything for nothing. In fact it's the fairest bet in the casino. Exactly 50/50. Like spinning a coin.

When you want to double your win simply press either the **double** or the **yes** button. A card will appear face-up on the screen. The other four cards will remain face down. Select the card that will be higher than the machine's card by pressing the button in front of it. If you are successful, the machine will always offer you another double until you lose or claim your win.

If your card is the same as the one chosen by the machine, its a draw and the game can proceed as normal.

It is really as simple as it sounds. Some players double when they get the urge, whereas other use the Video Poker machine purely as a gambling device. They double every win usually to a very high win, or bust.

To get at lot of money you have to win many doubles in succession - and of course stop before you lose! Your chances of being successful in succession are as follows:

NO OF DOUBLES	CHANCES	CASH IF R5 IS WAGERED
1	50%	$10
2	25%	$20
3	12,5%	$40
4	6,25%	$80
5	3,13%	$160
6	1,56%	$320
7	0,78%	$640
8	0,39%	$1280

Every double chance is 50% but from the above table, it is the sequence of wins on which you are actually gambling.

There are many different styles that players use. They seem to set rigid rules in their mind and play rather mechanically. To be totally flexible about deciding each time whether to double again can be very anxiety-provoking. The scientific way is to execute a predetermined number of doubles on wins of specific amounts.

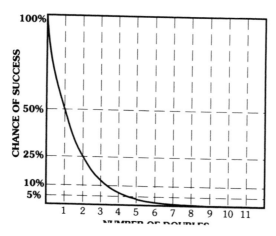

Let's say that the limit of your last double will be an amount over $500.

Starting with a pair of Jacks or higher (i.e. $5) it will take you 7 doubles. A chance of less than 1%.

127

Starting with $10 it will take you six doubles. Likewise starting with a full house win (i.e. $40) it will be four. That is eight times as possible.

We will recommend that, if doubling is your passion, double the highest wins you get four times if possible and bank the smaller wins as capital for playing on.

Some players think that the Poker machine is programmed to issue a high card when you want to double a big win. This is nonsense. The thought could only emanate from the shock at remembering the times you may have seen it happen. Ever tried to remember all the cards you got when you won?

THE ULTIMATE GAMBLER

One senior casino executive once advised me to stake the highest affordable stake on the wildest paying machine on a once off basis.

The closest equivalent to this in Video Poker would be to raid the highest denomination machine in the casino. Take the $100 machine that accepts three coins. This is ripe for a raid.

Decide before you play exactly what your strategy is going to be. Cash in three tokens and insert them all in the machine.

Whatever your win may be, cash out and leave. In the event of a money back win, know whether you will draw maximum credits or double a fixed number of times.

This is hair-raising stuff and really gets the adrenalin pumping. Who says it can't be your day to get a $240,000 Royal Flush? All this fun, hit and run, for $300—are you game?

128

SUPERSTITIONS 10

by PADDY GRAY

It could be said that the basis for gambling can be found in the genes of every homo sapiens. Primitive man believed that almost everything that happened to him was governed by outside forces. The natural elements exerted a strong influence on his behaviour and were a source of mystery and awe.

Men of ancient civilizations consulted the Oracles of Egypt, Greece and Rome as a normal, everyday occurrence. They considered the advice received to be the will of the gods which would direct their actions to the greatest advantage.

Even today, modern man makes many predictions as to future events in his life. For example—"I believe that I will get to the corner cafe and back before Uncle Jim telephones." Although few will admit to believing in Astrology many must get something from it, judging by the numbers of people who read their daily or monthly horoscopes in the press.

We all take risks every day of our lives—the prime example being that of driving a car, which we accept as part of our daily life. Does everyone not crave action in their lives—and could it not be said that everyone gambles in one way or another?

129

And don't we all believe in luck? "Good luck for the exams".... "Hope you have a lucky day". Maybe this is an unconscious challenge to calm our fears and anticipate pleasure and hope.

The Chinese in early Hong Kong days had a wonderful reason for the success of the Taipan; his Joss was fortunate. Everything he touched would turn to gold, because he was fortunate, or so the watchers believed. And in Greek mythology we have the Midas touch. Is that why so many punters drop a coin or two into the palm of the down-on-her-luck lady standing nearby, perhaps believing that this gesture will secure them the progressive jackpot that very night?

TO BE OR NOT TO BE—THAT IS THE QUESTION

The night has turned the corner well into the next morning and still the casino buzzes with "Great Expectations"—some tears; great excitement; some unbelievable good fortune.

On a bank of bonus 50¢ Video Poker machines the strident voice of a traditional "huisvrou" complains:

"Hierdie masjien vrek sonder siekte"
(This machine dies without sickness)

and the punters playing alongside collapse in a wonderfully warm feeling of camaraderie. Enough said—and all was said.

We are told that our opponent in a game of video poker is not made of flesh and blood. Our opponent is a machine, programmed for random selection. Yet hundreds of thousands of intelligent, rational players perform irrational and emotional rituals at the casino ... on the way to the casino ... selecting the day or night on which to visit the casino!!!

Is it courage that is needed to slay the monster in front of us? Is it a test of bravery when we engage the machine in

130

mental combat? Or is it the thrill of feeling alive when the spirit of adventure within us emerges and jungle justice prevails?

It's possible that the adrenalin surging through our own veins can be projected through our fingertips, transforming the metal beneath into a living opponent? What joy in conquest, what excitement then spurs on our eager desire to become instant millionaires.

Why otherwise would that dignified fellow dressed like a banker be sitting at a machine murmuring endearments ... "Talk to me baby, I know you understand my needs!"

"Hhmm..." chorus the three support spectators standing behind a friend who is dealt two pairs. "Yes! Yes!" They shriek their delight as this converts to a full house with the second draw. "Hhmm Hhmm..." They call out as a pair of Jacks are drawn with the next hand—followed by "Yes! Yes! Yes!" as this converted to a Trip. That is how easily a ritual is born. Here a group of players are operating on a *hunch*. They feel lucky and their combined instinct sees a relation between the chanting of "Hhmm" and a winning hand.

"But this machine only ever pays out a Straight Flush in Hearts" cry the indignant voices of the couple waiting their turn at their favorite machine—which is pouring out 500 coins for the player who has just turned up a Spades Straight Flush.

And further down the bank a couple are playing the end machine. Why is the end machine their lucky machine? Well, they have twice pulled out a Royal Flush on it. While he looks the other way she concentrates fiercely, while dropping five coins into the slot. The cards unfold; He turns to face the machine, selects and turns away again as she draws the final hand. Is that not the call sign for a Royal Flush?

131

Some rituals are performed with great concentration and intent; many have become so imprinted onto the player's subconscious mind that their origins are not remembered.

Let's listen in to some very common rituals that occur every night of the week, everywhere in the world.

THE RIGHT TIME TO VISIT A CASINO

"My left palm has been itching for days! Its telling me that I am sure to win a jackpot if I go gambling tonight."

"We are off to the Casino this evening. I hear you won the supermarket draw last week. May I rub your shoulder for luck?"

"What shall I wear? You know the last time that I was incredibly lucky I had on that old denim jacket—the one with glass studs. I did not have enough pockets though—maybe I should take my yellow moonbag as well. It has never let me down yet!"

"I will be in the car in a jiffy; I must just rub the silver candlestick Mother gave me. It always brought her good luck and it works for me too."

AND ... ON THE WAY TO THE CASINO

"Look there Fred ... A flock of birds before my eyes will certainly bring me a big surprise. I told you, I know it. We are definitely going to win today."

"Make a note of the first digit of the registration number of the next four cars that pass us. That will tell us what number machine to play on this evening."

"We have arrived—there is the casino sign on the right hand side of the road. Say hello—we are here to break a leg tonight."

132

AND FINALLY ... IN THE CASINO

"What is your lucky number? Six. See, here is machine number 2013. That adds up to six—and the last player was paid out 100 coins!"

"Nothing is working for me this evening. I cannot seem to get beyond 15 credits. Let's take time out and get a bite to eat. My luck is sure to change after dinner—I am always luckier after 9.00 p.m."

"Let's confuse the machine. We will put in 5 coins, then 4 coins, then three coins. Then when the machine's not looking we will play maximum coins for five minutes. This will work, I'm sure!"

"I never play with credits, it's unlucky. You know the machine is greedy and likes being fed with coins. You must cash out when you have fed in your wraps of coins and start again."

"Would you get me $50 worth of 50¢ wraps, but please make sure you get them from the first cashier from the left. She always gives me lucky money. And please don't put them in a container as the machine will think I am expecting to take away too much money and won't pay."

WILL LUCK BE A LADY TONIGHT?

I suspect that you've heard some of these superstitions. Maybe you have even performed the rituals yourself.

I know you will experience that marvelous sensation when the machine appears to be out running for you. Whatever your superstition or ritual, it's a comforting thought that it's not just you but Super You and the rabbit's foot which will exert an influence on your game and fortune this very day. After all, if coincidence happens more than once, is it still coincidence?

And here's a final thought to leave you with. Far more fortunate things might happen should you combine Super You, your precious rabbit's foot and the scientific mathematically-based options found in this book?

See you at the casino!!

QUIZ SECTION

Now is your chance to test your knowledge and discover how much you have learned. It is not advisable to embark on this quiz before you have absorbed and memorized the best selection options.

When you find yourself answering questions correctly, be sure that you are not guessing. That self deception would be self defeating and the value of the book would be lost.
It is also a summary and refresher that you could do time and again. Try it out on your friends who believe they are good at the game. You, and they, will soon know just how competent they are and whether any successes they may have had were blind luck.

It is just as important to claim the advantage of a small percentage with low value options as it is with the high values. There is already a percentage advantage in favor of the casino. Do not make it worse!

In the answer section, the percentage disadvantage has been calculated for you to understand the significance of a wrong selection. It is not presumed that you will be dealt the error hand all the time, although they do add up to going home early.

You are playing on a 6/5 machine (6 for Full House and 5 for a Flush) with a 1,000 payout for a Royal Flush. Which cards would you hold?
(Answers on page 177)

QUESTION 1

| A | B | C | D | E |

QUESTION 2

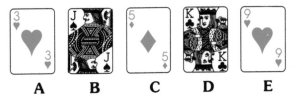

| A | B | C | D | E |

QUESTION 3

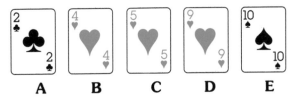

| A | B | C | D | E |

QUESTION 4

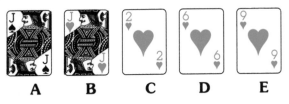

| A | B | C | D | E |

QUESTION 5

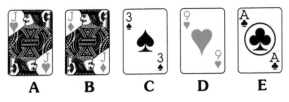

| A | B | C | D | E |

QUESTION 6

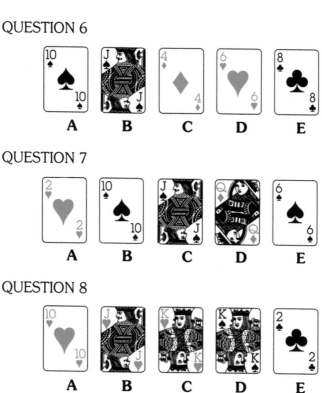

A   **B**   **C**   **D**   **E**

QUESTION 7

A   **B**   **C**   **D**   **E**

QUESTION 8

A   **B**   **C**   **D**   **E**

QUESTION 9

A   **B**   **C**   **D**   **E**

QUESTION 10

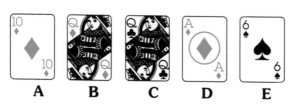

A   **B**   **C**   **D**   **E**

QUESTION 11

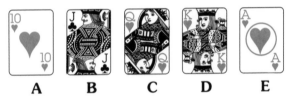

A   B   C   D   E

QUESTION 12

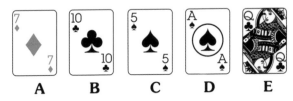

A   B   C   D   E

QUESTION 13

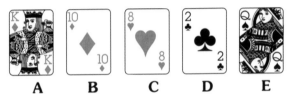

A   B   C   D   E

QUESTION 14

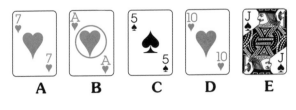

A   B   C   D   E

QUESTION 15

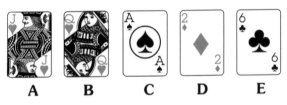

A   B   C   D   E

QUESTION 16

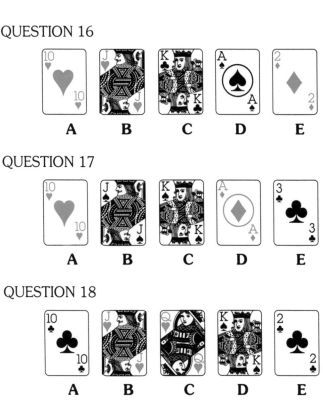

A   B   C   D   E

QUESTION 17

A   B   C   D   E

QUESTION 18

A   B   C   D   E

QUESTION 19

A   B   C   D   E

QUESTION 20

A   B   C   D   E

139

QUESTION 21

A   B   C   D   E

QUESTION 22

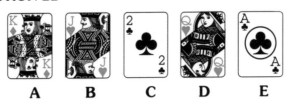

A   B   C   D   E

QUESTION 23

A   B   C   D   E

QUESTION 24

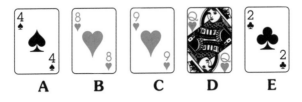

A   B   C   D   E

QUESTION 25

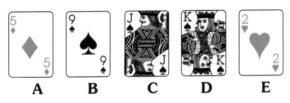

A   B   C   D   E

QUESTION 26

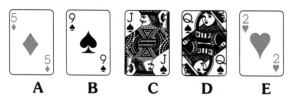

A   B   C   D   E

QUESTION 27

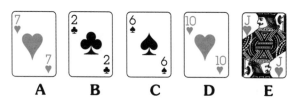

A   B   C   D   E

QUESTION 28

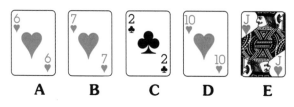

A   B   C   D   E

QUESTION 29

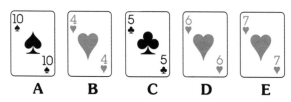

A   B   C   D   E

QUESTION 30

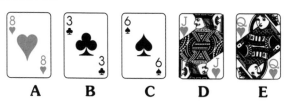

A   B   C   D   E

QUESTION 31

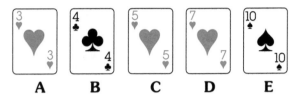

A   B   C   D   E

QUESTION 32

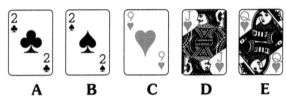

A   B   C   D   E

QUESTION 33

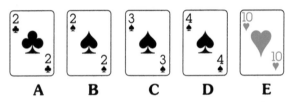

A   B   C   D   E

QUESTION 34

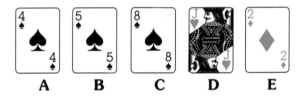

A   B   C   D   E

QUESTION 35

A   B   C   D   E

QUESTION 36

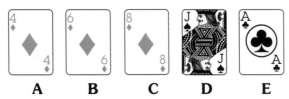

A   B   C   D   E

QUESTION 37

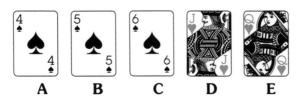

A   B   C   D   E

QUESTION 38

A   B   C   D   E

QUESTION 39

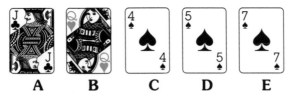

A   B   C   D   E

QUESTION 40

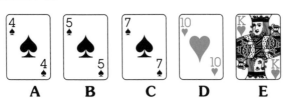

A   B   C   D   E

143

QUESTION 41

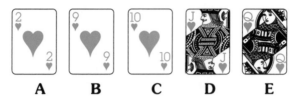

A **B** **C** **D** **E**

QUESTION 42

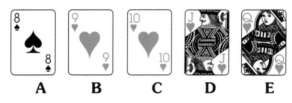

A **B** **C** **D** **E**

QUESTION 43

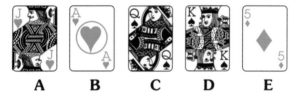

A **B** **C** **D** **E**

QUESTION 44

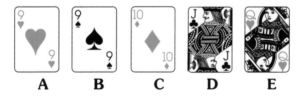

A **B** **C** **D** **E**

QUESTION 45

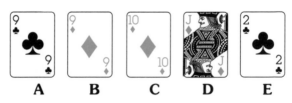

A **B** **C** **D** **E**

QUESTION 46

A   **B**   **C**   **D**   **E**

QUESTION 47

A   **B**   **C**   **D**   **E**

QUESTION 48

A   **B**   **C**   **D**   **E**

QUESTION 49

A   **B**   **C**   **D**   **E**

QUESTION 50

A   **B**   **C**   **D**   **E**

FACTS
& STATS

INTERPRETING THE QUIZ RESULTS

Firstly, you can check your score out of 50.

Secondly, you will not *just* get these hands dealt to you. many will be simply holding the odd picture card or a small pair. The quiz only includes the decision making examples. A good way to score is to add up the total percentage you have scored against you, then divide that figure by 50.

It will probably give you a higher percentage than you will experience in actual play but it is a guide.

Reasonable players can handle about 800 hands per hour. The amount of money put through a machine per hour is approximately as follows:

50¢ Machine	$2,000
$1 Machine	$4,000
$2 Machine	$8,000
$5 Machine	$20,000

That shows just how important the correct card selection must be. You can also, using the results of the quiz, easily calculate how much extra it is going to cost you per hour to play.

146

ANSWERS TO QUIZ

1. **A, B & C**
   Holding ABC & E is a 22% disadvantage
   Holding D & E is a 43% disadvantage

2. **B & D**
   Holding just B is a 7.5% disadvantage
   Holding just D is a 9.1% disadvantage

3. **REDEAL**
   Holding B, C & D is a 11.8% disadvantage

4. **A & B**
   Holding the four hearts is a 32.2% disadvantage

5. **A & B**
   Holding A, B & E is a 7.6% disadvantage

6. **A & B**
   To hold just B is a 10.1% disadvantage

7. **B & C**
   Holding B, C & D is a 5.4% disadvantage
   Holding C & D is a 0.2% disadvantage

8. **A, B & C**
   Holding C & D is a 4.6% disadvantage

9. **C & D**
   Holding A, B & C is a 3.7% disadvantage

10. **B & C**
    Holding A, B & D is a 2.9% disadvantage

11. **A, C, D & E**
    Holding all cards is a 82% disadvantage

12. **B & E**
    Holding D & E is a 1.2% disadvantage

13. **A & E**
Holding A & B is a 3.9% disadvantage

14. **B & E**
Holding B & D is a 4.8% disadvantage

15. **A & B**
Holding A, B & C is a 25.5% disadvantage

16. **A, B, C & D**
Holding A & B is a 7.9% disadvantage
Holding B, C & D is a 17.1% disadvantage

17. **B & C**
Holding A, B, C & D is a 10% disadvantage
Holding B, C & D is a 22.8% disadvantage

18. **A, B, C & D**
Holding B & C is a 30.5% disadvantage
Holding B, C & D is a 40.9% disadvantage

19. **B & E**
Holding A, B, C & D is a 8.3% disadvantage
Holding B, C & D is a 21.4% disadvantage

20. **B & C**
Holding A, B, C & D is a 7.2% disadvantage
Holding B, C & D is a 20.4% disadvantage

21. **A, B, C & D**
Holding B & D is a 3.9% disadvantage
Holding A & C is a 2% disadvantage

22. **B & D**
Holding A, B, D & E is a 1% disadvantage

23. **A, B & C**
Holding B, C & D is a 70% disadvantage

24. **B, C & D**
Holding D is a 8.6% disadvantage

25. **B, C & D**
Holding C & D is a 1.7% disadvantage

26. **B, C & D**
Holding C & D is a 15.3% disadvantage

27. **A, D & E**
Holding D & E is a 2.8% disadvantage

28. **A, B, D & E**
Holding A, B & D is a 60.8% disadvantage
Holding B, D & E is 50.8% disadvantage

29. **B, C, D & E**
Holding B, D & E is a 26.6% disadvantage

30. **D & E**
Holding A, D & E is a 1.3% disadvantage

31. **A, C & D**
Holding A, B, C & D is a 15% disadvantage

32. **A & B**
Holding C, D & E is a 11.9% disadvantage
Holding D & E is a 23.1% disadvantage

33. **A & B**
Holding B, C & D is a 24.7% disadvantage

34. **D**
Holding A, B & C is a 16% disadvantage

35. **A, B & C**
Holding D & E is a 13.9% disadvantage

36. **D & E**
Holding A, B & C is a 17.6% disadvantage

37. **D & E**
Holding A, B & C is a 5.6% disadvantage

38. **A, C & E**
Holding B & D is a 13.2% disadvantage

39. **A & B**
Holding C, D & E is a 2.9% disadvantage

40. **A, B & C**
Holding D & E is a 2% disadvantage

41. **HOLD ALL**
Holding B, C, D & E is a 29.8% disadvantage

42. **HOLD ALL**
Holding B, C, D & E is a 12.3% disadvantage

43. **A, B, C & D**
Holding A & B is a 3.9% disadvantage
Holding C & D is a 1.5% disadvantage

44. **B, C, D & E**
Holding A & B is a 2% disadvantage

45. **A & B**
Holding B, C & D is a 12.1% disadvantage

46. **A & B**
Holding A, B & C is a 6.7% disadvantage

47. **B & C**
Holding A & B is a 1% disadvantage

48. **B, C, D & E**
Holding A, B, C, D & E is a 78.9% disadvantage

49. **REDEAL**
Holding A, B, D & E is a 2.3% disadvantage

50. **A, B & D**
Holding B & C is a 2.6% disadvantage

150

BELOW WE HAVE REPRINTED A SELECTED LIST OF THE VALUES OF HOLD-ING CARDS WITH SPECIFIC DISCARDS. THEY ARE ARRANGED IN DESCEND-ING ORDER AND ARE QUOTED IN CENTS AND DECIMAL POINTS OF A CENT PER $1 WAGERED.

THE RESULTS FEATURED HERE ARE FROM THE 6/5 MACHINE WITH A 1,000 ROYAL FLUSH PAYOUT

HOLD	DISCARD	RESULT	HOLD	DISCARD	RESULT
10JQK S/S	1 S	2378.72	8 10J S/S	Q K D/S	57.91
JQKA S/S	1 S	2263.83	J A S/S	Q K D/S	57.30
10JQA S/S	1 S	2257.45	10JKA D/S	1 S	53.19
J J J D/S	X	411.93	J Q K D/S	2 S	51.53
777 D/S	X	411.93	10 J S/S	3 S	51.32
A A A D/S	X	411.93	J Q D/S	3 S	50.92
222 D/S	X	411.93	10 J S/S	Q D/S	50.24
9 10JQ S/S	1 S D/S	351.06	9 10K S/S	2 S D/S	50.23
8910J S/S	1 S D/S	344.68	2 3 4 S/S	2S D/S	49.95
78910 S/S	1 S D/S	338.30	4 5 7 S/S	2 S D/S	49.95
810JQ S/S	1S D/S	240.43	10 Q S/S	3 S	49.88
9JQK S/S	1 S D/S	236.17	J K D/S	3 S	49.74
2 PAIRS		234.04	Q K D/S	3 S	49.74
810JQ S/S	9 D/S	231.91	J Q D/S	K D/S	49.45
810JQ S/S	1 S D/S	229.79	J K D/S	10 D/S	48.95
7910J S/S	1 S D/S	223.40	Q K D/S	10 D/S	48.95
68910 S/S	1 S D/S	217.02	J Q K D/S	10 D/S	48.57
68910 S/S	A D/S	217.02	10 K S/S	3 S	48.44
J Q K S/S	2 S	167.81	10 Q S/S	J D/S	48.41
10JQ S/S	2 S	167.53	2 3 4 S/S	A D/S	48.20
J Q K S/S	A D/S	166.05	K A D/S	3/S	48.16
J Q K S/S	10 D/S	164.85	Q A D/S	3 S	48.16
10 JQ S/S	K D/S	164.29	J A D/S	3 S	48.16
J Q K S/S	6 S/S	163.64	J A D/S	10 D/S	47.76
10 JQ S/S	6 S/S	159.67	Q A D/S	10 D/S	47.76
Q K A S/S	2 S	158.09	K A D/S	10 D/S	47.76
J Q A S/S	2 S	158.09	J	4 S	47.59
10 JK S/S	2 S	157.82	10 JQ D/S	2 S D/S	47.46
J Q A S/S	10 D/S	156.61	Q	4 S	46.99
J Q A S/S	K D/S	156.34	10 K S/S	J D/S	46.97
Q K A S/S	J D/S	156.34	910QK D/S	1 S D/S	46.81
10 JK S/S	Q D/S	154.58	K	4 S	46.68
A A D/S	3 S D/S	150.60	10 A S/S	3 S	46.61
J J D/S	3 S D/S	150.60	A	4 S	46.43
10J A S/S	2 S	148.10	10 K S/S	9 S/S	46.41
A A 3	2 S	139.13	J	10 S/S	46.13
J J A	2 S	139.13	J	Q D/S	45.98
2JQA S/S	K D/S	114.89	Q	10 S/S	45.81
2JQA S/S	1 S D/S	114.89	Q K A D/S	2 S	45.61
24JQ S/S	1 S D/S	108.51	J Q A D/S	2 S	45.61
245J S/S	1 S D/S	102.13	Q	K D/S	45.52
2459 S/S	1 S D/S	95.74	K	10 S/S	45.48
10JQK D/S	1 S D/S	87.23	A	10 S/S	45.29
910JQ D/S	1 S D/S	80.85	K	J D/S	45.17
7 7 D/S	3 S D/S	79.32	10 JK D/S	2 S	41.54
2 2 D/S	3 S D/S	79.32	7910J D/S	1S D/S	40.43
8910J D/S	1 S D/S	74.47	4 5 8 S/S	J D/S	39.96
9 J Q S/S	2 S D/S	69.94	10 J D/S	3 S	39.36
9 10J S/S	2 S D/S	69.66	10 Q D/S	3 S	38.17
4567 S/S	1 S	68.09	910J D/S	2 S D/S	37.47
7 7 A	2 S	65.03	10 K D/S	3 S	36.99
2 2 A	2 S	65.03	8 J Q D/S	2 S D/S	35.62
J Q S/S	3 S	62.63	10 A D/S	3 S	35.41
J Q S/S	10 D/S	61.84	10 JA D/S	2 S	35.34
J K S/S	3 S	61.1	REDEAL	REDEAL	34.81
J Q S/S	K D/D	61.15	4568 D/S	1 S D/S	34.04
J Q S/S	8 S/	60.99	INITIAL	DEAL	33.09
9 J K S/S	2 S D/S	60.22	10	4 S	32.22
J Q S/S	K A D/S	60.17	9	4 S D/S	31.32
8 J Q S/S	K D/S	59.94	8	4 S D/S	31.15
8 10J S/S	2 S D/S	59.94	7	4 S D/S	31.04
J K S/S	Q D/S	59.72	6	4 S D/S	30.98
4 5 6 S/S	2 S D/S	59.67	4	4 S D/S	30.69
JQKA D/S	1 S	59.57	4 5 9 S/S	2 S D/S	30.53
J A S/S	3 S	59.36	3	4 S D/S	30.34
J K S/S	9 S/S	59.16	2	4 S D/S	29.99
J A S/S	10 D/S	58.96	4 5 6 D/S	2 S D/S	27.47
J K S/S	Q A D/S	58.44	4 9 S/S	3 S D/S	26.17
J A S/S	Q D/S	58.28	4 5 7 D/S	2 S D/S	21.55
J A S/S	10 Q D/S	57.98	4 5 8 D/S	2 S D/S	15.63
9 10Q S/S	K A D/S	57.91			

151

BELOW WE HAVE REPRINTED A SELECTED LIST OF THE VALUES OF HOLD-ING CARDS WITH SPECIFIC DISCARDS. THEY ARE ARRANGED IN DESCEND-ING ORDER AND ARE QUOTED IN CENTS AND DECIMAL POINTS OF A CENT PER $1 WAGERED.
THE RESULTS FEATURED HERE ARE FROM THE 9/6 MACHINE WITH A 1,000 ROYAL FLUSH PAYOUT

HOLD	DISCARD	RESULT	HOLD	DISCARD	RESULT
10JQK S/S	1 S	2393.6	JQKA D/S	1 S	59.6
JQKA S/S	1 S	2280.9	J A S/S	Q K D/S	59.0
10JQA S/S	1 S	2274.5	9 10K S/S	2 S D/S	54.3
J J J D/S	X	430.2	4 5 7 S/S	2 S D/S	53.9
777 D/S	X	430.2	2 3 4 S/S	2 S D/S	53.9
2 2 2 D/S	X	430.2	10JKA D/S	1 S	53.2
A A A D/S	X	430.2	10 J S/S	3 S	53.0
910JQ S/S	1 S D/S	366.0	2 3 4 S/S	A D/S	52.2
8910J S/S	1 S D/S	359.6	10 J S/S	Q D/S	51.9
78910 S/S	1 S D/S	353.2	J Q D/S	3 S	51.6
2 PAIR		259.6	10 Q S/S	3 S	51.5
810JQ S/S	1 S D/S	259.6	J Q K D/S	2 S	51.5
9JQK S/S	1 S D/S	253.2	J K D/S	3 S	50.4
810JQ S/S	9 D/S	251.1	Q K D/S	3 S	50.4
810JQ S/S	1 S D/S	246.8	10 K S/S	3 S	50.1
7910J S/S	1 S D/S	240.4	J Q D/S	K D/S	50.1
68910 S/S	1 S D/S	234.0	10 Q S/S	J D/S	50.1
68910 S/S	A D/S	234.0	Q K D/S	10 D/S	49.6
J Q K S/S	2 S	171.8	J K D/S	10 D/S	49.6
10JQ S/S	2 S	171.4	K A D/S	3 S	48.8
J Q K S/S	A D/S	170.0	J A D/S	3 S	48.8
J Q K S/S	10 D/S	168.8	Q A D/S	3 S	48.8
10 JQ S/S	K D/S	168.2	10 K S/S	J D/S	48.6
J Q K S/S	6 S/S	166.8	J Q K D/S	10 D/S	48.6
Q K A S/S	2 S	162.2	J A D/S	10 D/S	48.4
J Q A S/S	2 S	162.2	Q A D/S	10 D/S	48.4
10 JQ S/S	6 S/S	162.0	K A D/S	10 D/S	48.4
10 JK S/S	2 S	161.8	10 A S/S	3 S	48.3
J Q A S/S	10 D/S	160.7	J	4 S	48.3
J Q A S/S	K D/S	160.4	10 K S/S	9 D/S	47.8
Q K A S/S	J D/S	160.4	Q	4 S	47.7
10 JK S/S	Q D/S	158.6	10 JQ D/S	2 S D/S	47.5
A A D/S	3 S D/S	153.7	K	4 S	47.3
J J D/S	3 S D/S	153.7	A	4 S	47.1
10 J A S/S	2 S	152.2	910QK D/S	1 S D/S	46.8
J J A	2 S	141.6	J	10 S/S	46.7
A A 3	2 S	141.6	J	Q D/S	46.6
2JQA S/S	1 S D/S	134.0	Q	10 S/S	46.4
2JQA S/S	K D/S	134.0	Q	K D/S	46.2
24JQ S/S	1 S D/S	127.7	K	10 S/S	46.1
245J S/S	1 S D/S	121.3	A	10 S/S	45.9
2359 S/S	1 S D/S	114.9	K	J D/S	45.8
10JQK D/S	1 S D/S	87.2	J Q A D/S	2 S	45.6
7 7 D/S	3 S D/S	82.4	Q K A D/S	2 S	45.6
2 2 D/S	J Q K D/S	82.4	4 5 8 S/S	J D/S	44.0
2 2 D/S	3 S D/S	82.4	10 JK D/S	2 S	41.5
910JQ D/S	1 S D/S	80.9	9910J D/S	1 S D/S	40.4
9 J Q S/S	2 S D/S	73.9	10 J D/S	3 S	40.0
9 10J S/S	2 S D/S	73.5	10 Q D/S	3 S	38.8
4567 D.S	1 S	68.1	10 K D/S	3 S	37.7
7 7 A	2 S	67.5	910J D/S	2 S D/S	37.5
2 2 A	2 S	67.5	10 A D/S	3 S	36.1
9 J K S/S	2 S D/S	64.3	8 J Q D/S	2 S D/S	35.6
J Q S/S	3 S	64.3	10 JA D/S	2 S	35.3
8 J Q S/S	K D/S	64.0	REDEAL	REDEAL	35.3
810J S/S	2 S D/S	63.9	4 5 9 S/S	2 S D/S	34.7
4 5 6 S/S	2 S D/S	63.6	4568 D/S	1 S D/S	34.0
J Q S/S	10 D/S	63.5	INITIAL	DEAL	33.7
J K S/S	3 S	62.9	10	4 S	32.9
J Q S/S	K D/D	62.8	9	4 S D/S	32.0
J Q S/S	8 S/S	62.4	8	4 S D/S	31.8
9 10Q S/S	K A D/S	61.9	7	4 S D/S	31.7
8 10J S/S	Q K D/S	61.9	6	4 S D/S	31.7
JQ S/S	K A D/S	61.8	4	4 S D/S	31.4
J K S/S	Q D/S	61.4	3	4 S D/S	31.0
J A S/S	3 S	61.0	2	4 S D/S	30.7
J A S/S	10 D/S	60.6	4 9 S/S	3 S D/2	27.9
J K S/S	9 S/S	60.6	4 5 6 D/S	2 S D/S	27.5
J K S/S	Q A D/S	60.1	4 5 7 D/S	2 S D/S	21.6
J A S/S	Q D/S	60.0	4 5 8 D/S	2 S D/S	15.6
J A S/S	10 Q D/S	59.7			

BELOW WE HAVE REPRINTED A SELECTED LIST OF THE VALUES OF HOLD-
ING CARDS WITH SPECIFIC DISCARDS. THEY ARE ARRANGED IN DESCEND-
ING ORDER AND ARE QUOTED IN CENTS AND DECIMAL POINTS OF A CENT
PER $1 WAGERED.
THE RESULTS FEATURED HERE ARE FROM THE 7/5 MACHINE WITH A 800
ROYAL FLUSH PAYOUT AND PENALTY ACES AND SEVENS PAYING 80.

HOLD	DISCARD	RESULT	HOLD	DISCARD	RESULT
10JQK S/S	1 S	1953.2	J A S/S	10 Q D/S	57.3
JQKA S/S	1 S	1838.3	J A S/S	Q K D/S	56.6
10JQA S/S	1 S	1831.9	10JKA D/S	1 S	53.2
777 D/S	X	652.1	J Q K D/S	2 S	51.5
A A A D/S	X	652.1	J Q D/S	3 S	51.1
222 D/S	X	418.0	10 J S/S	3 S	50.3
J J J D/S	X	418.0	9 10K S/S	2 S D/S	50.2
910JQ S/S	1 S D/S	351.1	Q K D/S	3 S	50.0
8910J S/S	1 S D/S	344.7	J K D/S	3 S	50.0
78910 S/S	1 S D/S	338.3	457 S/S	2 S D/S	50.0
2 PAIR		242.6	234 S/S	2 S D/S	50.0
810JQ S/S	1 S D/S	240.4	J Q D/S	K D/S	49.7
9JQK S/S	1 S D/S	236.2	10 J S/S	Q D/S	49.2
810JQ S/S	9 D/S	231.9	Q K D/S	10 D/S	49.2
810JQ S/S	1 S D/S	229.8	J K D/S	10 D/S	49.2
7910J S/S	1 S D/S	223.4	10 Q S/S	3 S	48.9
68910 S/S	1 S D/S	217.0	Q A D/S	3 S	48.7
68910 S/S	A D/S	217.0	J A D/S	3 S	48.7
A A D/S	3 S D/S	166.9	K A D/S	3 S	48.7
J J D/S	3 S D/S	151.6	J Q K D/S	10 D/S	48.6
J Q K S/S	2 S	149.3	K A D/S	10 D/S	48.3
10JQ S/S	2 S	149.0	J A D/S	10 D/S	48.3
J Q K S/S	A D/S	147.5	Q A D/S	10 D/S	48.3
J Q K S/S	10 D/S	146.3	234 S/S	A D/S	48.2
10 JQ S/S	K D/S	145.8	A	4 S	47.8
J Q K S/S	6 S/S	145.1	J	4 S	47.7
A A 3	2 S	145.1	10 JQ D/S	2 S D/S	47.5
10 JQ S/S	6 S/S	141.2	10 K S/S	3 S	47.4
J J A	2 S	140.0	10 Q S/S	J D/S	47.4
Q K A S/S	2 S	139.6	Q	4 S	47.1
J Q A S/S	2 S	139.6	A	10 S/S	46.8
10 JK S/S	2 S	139.3	910QK D/S	1 S D/S	46.8
J Q A S/S	10 D/S	138.1	K	4 S	46.8
J Q A S/S	K D/S	137.8	J	10 S/S	46.3
Q K A S/S	J D/S	137.8	J	Q D/S	46.1
10 JK S/S	Q D/S	136.1	Q	10 S/S	46.0
10 J A S/S	2 S	129.6	10 K S/S	J D/S	46.0
2JQA S/S	1 S D/S	114.9	10 A S/S	3 S	45.9
2JQA S/S	K D/S	114.9	K	10 S/S	45.7
24JQ S/S	1 S D/S	108.5	Q	K D/S	45.6
245J S/S	1 S D/S	102.1	Q K A D/S	2 S	45.6
2459 S/S	1 S D/S	95.7	J Q A D/S	2 S	45.6
7 7 D/S	3 S D/S	95.6	10 K S/S	J D/S	45.4
10JQK D/S	1 S D/S	87.2	K	J D/S	45.3
910JQ D/S	1 S D/S	80.9	10J K D/S	2 S	41.5
2 2 D/S	3 S D/S	80.3	7910J D/S	1 S D/S	40.4
8910J D/S	1 S D/S	74.5	458 S/S	J D/S	40.0
7 7 A	2 S	71.0	10 J D D/S	3 S	39.6
9 J Q S/S	2 S D/S	69.9	10 Q D/S	3 S	38.4
9 10J S/S	2 S D/S	69.7	910J D/S	2 S D/S	37.5
4567 D/S	1 S	68.1	10 K D/S	3 S	37.2
2 2 A	2 S	65.9	10 A D/S	3 S	36.0
J Q S/S	3 S	61.6	8 J Q D/S	2 S D/S	35.6
J Q S/S	10 D/S	60.8	10 J A D/S	2 S	35.3
9 J K S/S	2 S D/S	60.2	REDEAL	REDEAL	35.1
J K S/S	3 S	60.2	4568 D/S	1 S D/S	34.0
J Q S/S	K D/D	60.1	INITIAL	DEAL	33.4
J Q S/S	8 S/S	60.0	7	4 S D/S	32.6
8 J Q S/S	K D/S	59.9	10	4 S	32.3
8 10J S/S	2 S D/S	59.9	9	4 S D/S	31.5
456 S/S	2 S D/S	59.7	8	4 S D/S	31.4
JQKA D/S	1 S	59.6	6	4 S D/S	31.2
J Q S/S	K A D/S	59.2	4	4 S D/S	30.9
J K S/S	Q D/S	58.7	3	4 S D/S	30.5
J A S/S	3 S	58.7	459 S/S	2 S D/S	30.5
J A S/S	10 D/S	58.3	2	4 S D/S	30.2
J K S/S	9 S/S	58.1	456 D/S	2 S D/S	27.5
9 10Q S/S	K A D/S	57.9	49 S/S	3 S D/S	26.4
8 10J S/S	Q K D/S	57.9	457 D/S	2 S D/S	21.6
J A S/S	Q D/S	57.6	458 D/S	2 S D/S	15.6
J K S/S	Q A D/S	57.4			

BELOW WE HAVE REPRINTED A SELECTED LIST OF THE VALUES OF HOLD-
ING CARDS WITH SPECIFIC DISCARDS. THEY ARE ARRANGED IN DESCEND-
ING ORDER AND ARE QUOTED IN CENTS AND DECIMAL POINTS OF A CENT
PER $1 WAGERED.
THE RESULTS FEATURED HERE ARE FROM THE 8/5 MACHINE WITH A 1,000
ROYAL FLUSH PAYOUT AND A STRAIGHT FLUSH PAYING 100.

HOLD	DISCARD	RESULT	HOLD	DISCARD	RESULT
10JQK S/S	1 S	2485.1	J K S/S	Q A D/S	59.2
JQKA S/S	1 S	2263.8	J A S/S	Q D/S	58.7
10JQA S/S	1 S	2257.4	J A S/S	10 Q D/S	58.4
910JQ S/S	A D/S	563.8	J A S/S	Q K D/S	57.7
8910J S/S	1 S D/S	557.4	2 3 4 S/S	A D/S	57.4
78910 S/S	1 S D/S	551.1	9 10K S/S	2 S D/S	54.9
2 2 2 D/S	X	424.1	10JKA D/S	1 S	53.2
A A A D/S	X	424.1	10 J S/S	3 S	52.7
7 7 7 D/S	X	424.1	10 J S/S	Q D/S	51.6
J J J D/S	X	424.1	J Q K D/S	2 S	51.5
810JQ S/S	1 S D/S	346.8	JQ D/S	3 S	51.4
9JQK S/S	1 S D/S	342.6	10 Q S/S	3 S	50.9
810JQ S/S	9 D/S	338.3	Q K D/S	3 S	50.2
810JQ S/S	1 S D/S	336.2	J K D/S	3 S	50.2
7910J S/S	1 S D/S	329.8	J Q D/S	K D/S	49.9
68910 S/S	1 S D/S	323.4	10 Q S/S	J D/S	49.5
68910 S/S	1 D/S	323.4	Q K D/S	10 D/S	49.4
2 PAIR		251.1	J K D/S	10 D/S	49.4
10JQ S/S	2 S	176.8	10 K S/S	3 S	49.2
10 JQ S/S	K D/S	173.5	J A D/S	3 S	48.6
J Q K S/S	2 S	172.4	K A D/S	3 S	48.6
J Q K S/S	A D/S	170.7	Q A D/S	3 S	48.6
J Q K S/S	10 D/S	169.5	J Q K D/S	10 D/S	48.6
10 JQ S/S	6 S/S	168.9	Q A D/S	10 D/S	48.2
J Q K S/S	6 S/S	168.3	K A D/S	10 D/S	48.2
10 JK S/S	2 S	162.4	J A D/S	10 D/S	48.2
10 JK S/S	Q D/S	159.2	J	4 S	48.0
Q K A S/S	2 S	158.1	10 K S/S	J D/S	47.7
J Q A S/S	2 S	158.1	10 JQ D/S	2 S D/S	47.5
J Q A S/S	10 D/S	156.6	Q	4 S	47.4
Q K A S/S	J D/S	156.3	10 A S/S	3 S	47.1
J Q A S/S	K D/S	156.3	K	4 S	47.0
A A D/S	3 S D/S	152.6	10 K S/S	9 D/S	46.9
J J D/S	3 S D/S	152.6	910QK D/S	1 S D/S	46.8
10 J A S/S	2 S	148.1	A	4 S	46.8
A A 3	2 S	140.8	J	10 S/S	46.5
J J A	2 S	140.8	J	Q D/S	46.4
2JQA S/S	1 S D/S	114.9	Q	10 S/S	46.1
2JQA S/S	K D/S	114.9	Q	K D/S	45.9
24JQ S/S	1 S D/S	108.5	K	10 S/S	45.8
245J S/S	1 S D/S	102.1	A	10 S/S	45.6
2459 S/S	1 S D/S	95.7	J Q A D/S	2 S	45.6
10JQK D/S	1 S D/S	87.2	Q K A D/S	2 S	45.6
9 10J S/S	2 S D/S	83.5	K	J D/S	45.5
7 7 D/S	3 S D/S	81.4	4 5 8S/S	J D/S	44.6
2 2 D/S	3 S D/S	81.4	10 JK D/S	2 S	41.5
910JQ D/S	1 S D/S	80.9	7910J D/S	1 S D/S	40.4
9 J Q S/S	2 S D/S	79.2	10 J D/S	3 S	39.8
8910J D/S	1 S D/S	74.5	10 Q D/S	3 S	38.6
4 5 6 S/S	2 S D/S	73.5	910J D/S	2 S D/S	37.5
8 10J S/S	2 S D/S	69.2	10 K D/S	3 S	37.4
4567 D/S	1 S	68.1	10 A D/S	3 S	35.9
8 10J S/S	Q K D/S	67.2	8 J Q D/S	2 S D/S	35.6
9 10Q S/S	K A D/S	67.2	10 JA D/S	2 S	35.3
2 2 A	2 S	66.7	REDEAL	REDEAL	35.1
7 7 A	2 S	66.7	4568 D/S	1 S D/S	34.0
9 J K S/S	2 S D/S	64.8	INITIAL	DEAL	33.4
8 J Q S/S	K D/S	64.6	10	4 S	32.7
J Q S/S	3 S	63.7	9	4 S D/S	31.7
J Q S/S	10 D/S	62.9	8	4 S D/S	31.6
J Q S/S	K D/D	62.2	7	4 S D/S	31.4
J K S/S	3 S	61.9	6	4 S D/S	31.4
J Q S/S	8 S/S	61.7	4	4 S D/S	31.1
J Q S/S	K A D/S	61.2	3	4 S D/S	30.7
J K S/S	Q D/S	60.5	4 5 9 S/S	2 S D/S	30.5
J A S/S	3 S	59.8	2	4 S D/S	30.4
J K S/S	9 S/S	59.6	4 5 6 D/S	2 S D/S	27.5
JQKA D/S	1 S	59.6	4 9 S/S	3 S D/S	26.6
J A S/S	10 D/S	59.4	4 5 7 D/S	2 S D/S	21.6
4 5 7 S/S	2 S D/S	59.2	4 5 8 D/S	2 S D/S	15.6
2 3 4 S/S	2S D/S	59.2			

BELOW WE HAVE REPRINTED A SELECTED LIST OF THE VALUES OF HOLD-
ING CARDS WITH SPECIFIC DISCARDS. THEY ARE ARRANGED IN DESCEND-
ING ORDER AND ARE QUOTED IN CENTS AND DECIMAL POINTS OF A CENT
PER $1 WAGERED.
THE RESULTS FEATURED HERE ARE FROM THE 7/5 MACHINE WITH A 800
ROYAL FLUSH PAYOUT AND PENALTY ACES PAYING 80 AND 2'S 3'S & 4'S 40.

HOLD	DISCARD	RESULT	HOLD	DISCARD	RESULT
10JQK S/S	1 S	1953.2	J A S/S	10 Q D/S	57.3
JQKA S/S	1 S	1838.3	J A S/S	Q K D/S	56.6
10JQA S/S	1 S	1831.9	10JKA D/S	1 S	53.2
A A A D/S	X	652.1	J Q K D/S	2 S	51.5
2 2 2 D/S	X	481.9	J Q D/S	3 S	51.1
7 7 7 D/S	X	418.0	10 J S/S	3 S	50.3
J J J D/S	X	418.0	9 10K S/S	2 S D/S	50.2
910JQ S/S	1 S D/S	351.1	Q K D/S	3 S	50.0
8910J S/S	1 S D/S	344.7	J K D/S	3 S	50.0
78910 S/S	1 S D/S	338.3	4 5 7 S/S	2 S D/S	50.0
2 PAIR		242.6	2 3 4 S/S	2 S D/S	50.0
810JQ S/S	1 S D/S	240.4	J Q D/S	K D/S	49.7
9JQK S/S	1 S D/S	236.2	10 J S/S	Q D/S	49.2
810JQ S/S	9 D/S	231.9	Q K D/S	10 D/S	49.2
810JQ S/S	1 S D/S	229.8	J K D/S	10 D/S	49.2
7910J S/S	1 S D/S	223.4	10 Q S/S	3 S	48.9
68910 S/S	1 S D/S	217.0	Q A D/S	3 S	48.7
68910 S/S	A D/S	217.0	J A D/S	3 S	48.7
A A D/S	3 S D/S	166.9	K A D/S	3 S	48.7
J J D/S	3 S D/S	151.6	J Q K D/S	10 D/S	48.6
J Q K S/S	2 S	149.3	K A D/S	10 D/S	48.3
10JQ S/S	2 S	149.0	J A D/S	10 D/S	48.3
J Q K S/S	A D/S	147.5	Q A D/S	10 D/S	48.3
J Q K S/S	10 D/S	146.3	2 3 4 S/S	A D/S	48.2
10 JQ S/S	K D/S	145.8	A	4 S	47.8
J Q K S/S	6 S/S	145.1	J	4 S	47.7
A A 3	2 S	145.1	10 JQ D/S	2 S D/S	47.5
10 J Q S/S	6 S/S	141.2	10K S/S	3 S	47.4
J J A	2 S	140.0	10 Q S/S	J D/S	47.4
Q K A S/S	2 S	139.6	Q	4 S	47.1
J Q A S/S	2 S	139.6	A	10 S/S	46.8
10 JK S/S	2S	139.3	910QK D/S	1 S D/S	46.8
J Q A S/S	10 D/S	138.1	K	4 S	46.8
J Q A S/S	K D/S	137.8	J	10 S/S	46.3
Q K A S/S	J D/S	137.8	J	Q D/S	46.1
10 J K S/S	Q D/S	136.1	Q	10 S/S	46.0
10 J A S/S	2 S	129.6	10 K S/S	J D/S	46.0
2JQA S/S	1 S D/S	114.9	10 A S/S	3 S	45.9
2JQA S/S	K D/S	114.9	K	10 S/S	45.7
24JQ S/S	1 S D/S	108.5	Q	K D/S	45.6
245J S/S	1 S D/S	102.1	Q K A D/S	2 S	45.6
2459 S/S	1 S D/S	95.7	J Q A D/S	2 S	45.6
10JQK D/S	1 S D/S	87.2	10 K S/S	9 D/S	45.4
2 2 D/S	3 S D/S	84.5	K	J D/S	45.3
910JQ D/S	1 S D/S	80.9	10 JK D/S	2 S	41.5
7 7 D/S	3 S D/S	80.3	7910J D/S	1 S D/S	40.4
8910J D/S	1S D/S	74.5	4 5 8 S/S	J D/S	40.0
9 J Q S/S	2 S D/S	69.9	10 J D/S	3 S	39.6
9 10J S/S	2 S D/S	69.7	10 Q D/S	3 S	38.4
4567 S/S	1 S	68.1	910J D/S	2 S D/S	37.5
2 2 A	2 S	67.3	10 K D/S	3 S	37.2
7 7 A	2 S	65.9	10 A D/S	3 S	36.0
J Q S/S	3 S	61.6	8 J Q D/S	2 S D/S	35.6
J Q S/S	10 D/S	60.8	10 J A D/S	2 S	35.3
9 J K S/S	2 S D/S	60.2	REDEAL	REDEAL	35.1
J K S/S	3 S	60.2	4568 D/S	1 S D/S	34.0
J Q S/S	K D/D	60.1	INITIAL	DEAL	33.4
J Q S/S	8 S/S	60.0	10	4 S	32.3
8 J Q S/S	K D/S	59.9	9	4 S D/S	31.5
8 10J S/S	2 S D/S	59.9	8	4 S D/S	31.4
4 5 6 S/S	2 S D/S	59.7	4	4 S D/S	31.3
JQKA D/S	1 S	59.6	7	4 S D/S	31.2
J Q S/S	K A D/S	59.2	6	4 S D/S	31.2
J K S/S	Q D/S	58.7	3	4 S D/S	30.9
J A S/S	3 S	58.7	2	4 S D/S	30.6
J A S/S	10 D/S	58.3	4 5 S/S	2 S D/S	30.5
J K S/S	9 S/S	58.1	4 5 6 D/S	2 S D/S	27.5
9 10Q S/S	K A D/S	57.9	4 9 S/S	3 S D/S	26.5
8 10J S/S	Q K D/S	57.9	4 5 7 D/S	2 S D/S	21.6
J A S/S	Q D/S	57.6	4 5 8 D/S	2 S D/S	15.6
J K S/S	Q A D/S	57.4			

155

HOW IS YOUR LUCK?

Sometimes you think you are having a run of bad luck in as much as, at other times, you may not realize that you were going through a purple patch. Just to get the average possibilities into perspective, here is a list of just how often certain combinations should be attained. More, or less often, will tell you just how your luck is running.

Holding a pair will convert into

2 pairs	every 6 times held
Trip	every 9 times held
Full House	every 98 times held
Penalties	every 360 times held
Something better	every 4.8 times held

Holding a trip will convert into:

Full House	every 16 times held
Penalties	every 23 times held
something better	every 10 times held

2 pairs will convert into a Full house every 12 times held

Holding 4 of a Royal Flush will convert every 47 times held
3 of a Royal Flush will convert every 1,081 times held
2 of a Royal Flush will convert every 16,215 times held
1 of a Royal Flush will convert every 178,365 times held
Being dealt a Royal Flush will happen every 649,740 times
Being dealt a Royal Flush (in Spades) every 2,598,960 times

holding 4 of a flush will covert every 5.2 times (not 1 in 4!)
holding 3 of a flush will convert every 25 times

3 of a Closed Straight Flush will convert every 1,081 times
3 of a Half Open Straight Flush will convert every 540 times
3 of a Open Straight Flush will convert every 360 times

Holding 3 of an Open Straight Flush will convert into a Straight Flush the same number of times as a pair will convert into penalties!

Holding one picture card will convert into a Pr of Jacks or higher every 3.9 times
Holding two picture cards will convert into a Pr of Jacks or higher every 3.2 times
Holding three picture cards will convert into a Pr of Jacks or higher every 3.1 times
Holding 4 picture cards will convert into a Pr of Jacks or higher every 3.9 times
(Almost the same chance of holding 1 or 4 picture cards excluding the straight)

THESE FIGURES ARE AVERAGE AND WILL HAPPEN
"IN THE FULLNESS OF TIME"

A progressive machine, available in almost every casino.
(Courtesy Casino Player, *the magazine for gaming*
enthusiasts.)

You have had some wonderful experiences playing Video Poker. You can probably relate many stories of record jackpots and interesting incidents that have occurred. You may even be able to add to the list of habits, rituals and superstitions that are associated with Video Poker. Also, you may have had sets of cards dealt to you that were hard to fathom.

If you have any of these to share with us, we would appreciate hearing from you.

Here's our address:

Citadel Press
600 Madison Ave.
New York, NY
10022

ENJOY!

Gambling Books Ordering Information

Ask for any of the books listed below at your bookstore. Or to order direct from the publisher, call 1-800-447-BOOK (MasterCard or Visa), or send a check or money order for the books purchased (plus $4.00 shipping and handling for the first book ordered and $1.00 for each additional book) to Carol Publishing Group, 120 Enterprise Avenue, Dept. 1605, Secaucus, NJ 07094.

Beating the Wheel: The System That's Won More Than $6 Million, From Las Vegas to Monte Carlo by Russell T. Barnhart
$12.95 paper   0-8184-0553-8   (CAN $15.95)

Beat the House: Sixteen Ways to Win at Blackjack, Craps, Roulette, Baccarat and Other Table Games by Frederick Lembeck
$12.95 paper   0-8065-1607-0   (CAN $17.95)

Blackjack Your Way to Riches by Richard Albert Canfield
$9.95 paper   0-8184-0498-1   (CAN $12.95)

The Body Language of Poker: Mike Caro's Book of Tells by Mike Caro
$18.95 paper   0-89746-100-2   (CAN $23.95)

Caro on Gambling by Mike Caro
$6.95 paper   0-89746-029-4   (CAN $9.95)

The Cheapskate's Guide to Las Vegas: Hotels, Gambling, Food, Entertainment, and Much More by Connie Emerson
$9.95 paper   0-8065-1530-9   (CAN $13.95)

The Complete Guide to Riverboat Gambling: It's History, and How to Play, Win and Have Fun by Scott Faragher
$12.95 paper   0-8065-1569-4   (CAN $17.95)

Darwin Ortiz on Casino Gambling: The Complete Guide to Playing and Winning by Darwin Ortiz
$12.95 paper   0-8184-0525-2   (CAN $16.95)

Gambling Scams: How They Work, How to Detect Them, How to Protect Yourself by Darwin Ortiz
$10.95 paper   0-8184-0529-5   (CAN $14.95)

Gambling Times Guide to Blackjack by Stanley Roberts
$9.95 paper   0-89746-015-4   (CAN $12.95)

Gambling Times Guide to Craps by N.B. Winkless
$9.95 paper   0-89746-013-8   (CAN $12.95)

How to be Treated Like a High Roller by Robert Renneisen
$7.95 paper   0-8184-0556-2   (CAN $9.95)

How To Win at Casino Gaming Tournaments by Haven Earle Haley
$8.95 paper   0-89746-016-2   (CAN $11.95)

John Patrick's Blackjack
$12.95 paper   0-8184-0555-4   (CAN $16.95)

John Patrick's Craps
$14.95 paper   0-8184-0554-6   (CAN $18.95)

John Patrick's Slots
$12.95 paper   0-8184-0574-0   (CAN $15.95)

The Mathematics of Gambling by Edward O. Thorp
$7.95 paper   0-89746-019-7   (CAN $10.95)

Million Dollar Blackjack by Ken Uston
$16.95 paper   0-89746-068-5   (CAN $21.95)

New Poker Games by Mike Caro
$5.95 paper   0-89746-040-5   (CAN $7.95)

Playing Blackjack as a Business by Lawrence Revere
$14.95 paper   0-8184-0064-1   (CAN $18.95)

Progression Blackjack: Exposing the Cardcounting Myth by Donald Dahl
$8.95 paper 0-8065-1396-9 (CAN $10.95)

Psyching Out Vegas: Winning Through Psychology in the Casinos of the World by Marvin Karlins, Ph.D.
$15.00 cloth   0-914314-03-3   (CAN $19.95)

Win at Video Poker: The Guide to Beating the Poker Machines by Roger Fleming
$9.95 paper   0-8065-1605-4   (CAN $13.95)

Winning at Slot Machines by Jim Regan
$5.95 paper   0-8065-0973-2   (CAN $7.95)

Winning Blackjack in Atlantic City and Around the World by Thomas Gaffney
$7.95 paper   0-8065-1178-8   (CAN $10.95)

Winning Blackjack Without Counting Cards by David S. Popik
$7.95 paper   0-8065-0963-5   (CAN $10.95)

(Prices subject to change; books subject to availability)